the grand tea master

a biography of Hounsai Soshitsu Sen XV

by Herbert Plutschow

The photograph on the title page shows Hounsai preparing tea
under the supervision of his father Tantansai.

First edition, 2001

Published by Weatherhill, Inc.
41 Monroe Turnpike
Trumbull, CT 06611

Library of Congress Cataloging-in-Publication Data available upon request.

CONTENTS

A s I was writing this book, Sen Tomiko, Hounsai's wife of forty-four years, died unexpectedly of heart failure on March 9, 1999, at the age of sixty-eight. For twenty years, Mrs. Sen had served as president of the Japanese chapter of Soroptimist International and as head of the Urasenke Gakuen school. While she was in the hospital, France awarded her the medal Chevalier, but she was unable to attend the celebration party.

With her fluency in English and French, Mrs. Sen contributed to her husband's work to internationalize tea and conversed with many of the world leaders, including France's Jacques Chirac and Mikhail and Raisa Gorbachev, when they visited Urasenke. Her major achievement, however, was to elevate the position of *iemoto* wife at Urasenke and to alleviate the weight of feudalism that deprived wives of any official public functions in tea. She authored a book on the history of tea sweets and published her autobiographical *Mune no Komichi* (The Trail of My Heart) in 1974.

This book is dedicated to her memory.

part one

Grand Tea Master Hounsai's Inheritance

Introduction

Grand Tea Master Hounsai[1] was born in 1923 in Kyoto, the fifteenth descendant of the great tea master Sen Rikyu (1522–91), who is revered as the founder of most modern schools of tea. Like all his fourteen pre-decessors, Hounsai dedicated his life to the preservation of the tea traditions he inherited, and to sustaining tea's popularity inside Japan. He is unique in that he has also worked very hard to introduce tea outside Japan, with remarkable success. In recognition of his contributions to tea and, through tea, to Japanese culture, the emperor of Japan awarded him the Medal of Culture in 1996, the highest honor the emperor can give to a subject for his or her outstanding cultural achievements.

I have known Hounsai for almost two decades, both as a leader of traditional culture and, at the same time, as a cosmopolitan. In a sense, he is an ideal citizen of the world, who meets other cultures with an exceptional openness while retaining a strong Japanese identity. Hounsai is a complex personality, reflecting Japan's complex role in the world of the twentieth century. He is the product of tea history and traditions, as well as of a rapidly changing world. He also represents the efforts all his predecessors have made to preserve the essence of the tea tradition regardless of the changes that continually swept the country in the course of its history. Hounsai represents more than just himself; he deserves a book.

In seeking to convey a better understanding of tea and the role of a grand tea masters (*iemoto*) in modern Japanese culture and society, this book goes beyond simple biography. My aim is to provide insight into the tea traditions and philosophy that Hounsai has been called upon to cherish and to transmit to future generations. One must constantly refer to that culture to understand Hounsai's life and activities. We cannot isolate him from his cultural environment and the history in which he lives.

This is always true in biography, but even more so in this case, for Hounsai is more than a mere individual; he is an institution.

As Hounsai culminates a long tradition of tea and past generations of tea masters, we must examine each aspect of this tradition: tea philosophy, tea ritual, tea aesthetics, and the Way of Tea and the iemoto system through history up to Hounsai. In each of these categories we will give him the first and the last word. This approach is not without its drawbacks. If it appears to the reader at times that there is too much on tea and too little on the grand master, then he or she must realize that this book treats the grand master not merely as an individual but also as a tea master who embodies tea's long history and complex philosophy. Although some of this background may seem unrelated to the grand master, I want the reader to see it as part of the institution that the grand master represents. Hounsai embodies and lives the entire scope of the tea tradition this book presents.

The most prominent and influential of Hounsai's predecessors in the long tradition of tea are Murata Juko (1423–1502), Takeno Jo'o (1502–55), Sen Rikyu (1522–91), and Sen Sotan (1578–1658). These names will appear often in this account, because it was these men who shaped Japanese tea as we know it today. Without these towering figures, Japanese tea would be quite different, or it would no longer exist. Many traditional arts have not survived. Perhaps they lost their sponsors and popular support due to historic change, or the artists did not have personalities strong enough to ensure continuing sponsorship. It may also be that the masters of these traditional arts were too inflexible and unable to cope with the modern world. At crucial moments of history, tea was blessed with strong personalities who had the vision to adapt the tradition to the changing times. Hounsai is certainly one of them.

Tea is difficult to define because it is a complex art. "Tea is highly eclectic," writes Hounsai, "combining religion, philosophy, ethics, aesthetics, and praxis. It is simplicity, asymmetry, refinement, naturalness, mystery, otherworldliness, and tranquility." [2] Others have described it as a household sacrament or as a performing art. For some it provides the means for artistic display. Because of its involvement with Zen Buddhism, some take it as a path toward religious enlightenment or "salvation through beauty." Today tea is a repository of traditional Japanese art, taste, modes of social intercourse, and a continuing source of spiritual and aesthetic pleasure. It also continues to nurture the cultural identity of many Japanese.

I have used the word tea instead of the Japanese *cha* (tea) or *chanoyu* (Way of Tea) or the capitalized Tea. To emphasize spirituality over formality, Hounsai prefers chanoyu over "tea ceremony." Rather than using another Japanese term in a text already overburdened with Japanese names and terms, I chose instead to use tea in the lowercase to indicate tea as a beverage, as a philosophy, an aesthetic, a discipline, and a ritual. The context makes it sufficiently clear what is meant in each case.

I have italicized on first appearance all Japanese terms not appearing in *Webster's Third International Dictionary*, while leaving those that do—for example, tatami and kimono—in Roman letters. I have capitalized the names of tea huts and rooms and theater genres (Noh, Kyogen, Kabuki). I have placed quotation marks around names of tea utensils, as is the convention for works of art, and the titles of Zen parables.

Until the introduction of the solar calendar on November 9, 1872, Japanese dates herein follow the lunar calendar.

My main sources for Hounsai's life and thought was an interview he granted me in the summer of 1998, his autobiography *Ocha o Dozo—Watakushi no Rirekisho* (1987) and *Cha no Shintai* (1980), as well as the articles he wrote in each of the issues of the journal *Chanoyu Quarterly* and *Tanko*.

Until recently, the study of tea has been the domain of scholars specializing in the art and cultural history of the Ashikaga (also Muromachi) period (1336–1573). In the postwar period, tea began attracting the attention of Western scholars. *Tea in Japan*, published in 1989 by University of Hawaii Press and sponsored by Hounsai, attests to the high level of scholarly interest tea has attracted in the West. Japanese and Western scholars have studied tea according to various academic disciplines and approaches: historical, anthropological, and sociological. Few scholars, however, have looked at tea from the point of view of comparative religion or, more specifically, of comparative ritual. I have adopted this approach as my principal methodology, supplementing it when necessary with other methods of analysis. The iemoto system, for example, requires a multidisciplinary analysis, although it does manifest, especially in its early development, a religio-ritual dimension. What tea has in common with the earliest known human rituals is that aspect of communal feasting which is also called the ritual banquet. Such rituals were used in ancient civilizations as means to commune with the divine as well as to consolidate the human order. Scholars have also elaborated on the economic aspects of these ancient banquets, which involve equal distribution of ritual food (meat) among all participants. Japanese tea, however, uses equal ritual distribution as a Buddhist token of human equality, rather than as an economic ritual.

A Typical Tea Meeting Hosted by Hounsai

"Tea" is without doubt one of the most frequently used words in this book. It is therefore necessary, before proceeding further, to provide the reader with an idea of how Hounsai invites and serves tea to his guests. It is doubtful that Hounsai would invite his guests without the intention of serving them a full tea course—that is, food, sweets, and thick and thin tea, in that order.

What follows is a description of a typical tea meeting to which Hounsai, or any other accomplished tea master, invites ordinary people (as opposed to state guests or other high dignitaries). Customarily, tea begins with the host sending out invitations to his guests to come to his tea meeting at a certain day and time. The invitees must confirm their willingness to attend because a tea meeting requires minute and painstaking preparations. The guests are also supposed to dress in their best, and to avoid wearing strong perfumes or jewelry, which may scratch precious tea utensils. Hounsai expects his guests to know how to proceed to the tea room through the *roji* path, how to wash their hands and rinse their mouths at the water basin, how to enter the tea room through the small *nijiriguchi* entrance, how to view the flower and calligraphy display in the tokonoma alcove, and how to seat themselves in the order Hounsai has determined (main guest, or *shokyaku*; second guest, or *jikyaku*; and last guest, or *otsume*). The main guest must sit near the alcove, the spot closest to the all-sacred tokonoma of the tea room and the *temaeza*, the place where the host prepares the tea. Before the appointed hour, the host unlocks the garden gate and bids his guests to enter, but lets them proceed by themselves over the freshly sprinkled stepping stones that lead to the waiting parlor. All guests arrive at about the same time; they pass through the outer gate and enter the entryway, where they change their shoes and take off their wraps. Then they proceed to the waiting room, where each is served hot water in a small cup. The guests then move to a sheltered waiting parlor at the edge of a small garden. Quiet, unpretentious, and modeled after a mountain trail far away from any city, the moss-covered path with its natural-looking stepping stones leads the guests to the tea hut. Once they proceed along this path, the guests leave their everyday concerns behind. With its unpainted wooden posts and lintels, wattle walls, and thatched or bark roof, the tea hut suggests a mountain retreat, perfectly blending into the natural surroundings. The guests proceed to the parlor, sit down, and enjoy the trees and bushes and the garden stones, arranged to convey the impression of a rustic mountain scene. The guests wait in the parlor until the host appears, silently greeting them. This greeting is the sign for the guests to proceed, one by one, along the path toward the tea hut. Before entering the hut, however, each guest must wash his hands and rinse his mouth in a symbolic act of purification. Then, again one by one, the guests crawl into the hut through the small nijiriguchi entrance. The purpose of this entrance is "to humble oneself . . . to abandon one's worldly status completely," wrote Hounsai.[3]

Once inside the tea room, each guest proceeds to the tokonoma alcove to admire the flower or scroll displayed in it; in this case Hounsai has displayed a single morning glory in a bamboo vase of his own design. Then they inspect the hearth, kettle, and the charcoal burning in the neatly shaped ash. After they have had a good look at the room, its walls, ceiling, and paper windows, they sit down. The host will not enter the tearoom until the guests have all sat down. Orientation in a tea room is an important part of tea training and behavior. When everyone is seated, the host enters through an inner door and thanks his guests for honoring such a humble hut with their presence. The guests in turn thank the host for the invitation. They converse seriously and modestly on wholesome topics for a short time. Then the host places more charcoal in the fire (*shozumi*), and the incense in the fire fills the room with a pleasant fragrance.[4]

The host then returns to the preparation room to bring in the food. He serves a simple meal of liquid and solid foods, some selected from the mountains and others from the sea. Like the flowers in the alcove, the food is seasonal and fresh. It is served on small trays that the host places in front of each guest. It is important that the food be presented in an aesthetically pleasing manner; it must please the eyes as well as the palate. The food is thus "tasted" in three ways, according to Hounsai, "with eyes, tongue, and heart." The chopsticks are made of freshly cut green bamboo. The host reappears from time to time to ask the guests if they want more to eat and to serve them saké. When all the guests have finished, they clean their dishes with the tissue paper they are expected to bring to a tea meeting and place them neatly at the place where they received them.

After the host has cleared away the trays, the guests go out into the garden to stretch their legs. While the guests are in the garden, the host reenters, arranges fresh flowers, and hangs a new scroll in the alcove. He then strikes a gong or a wooden board to announce to his guests that they may now reenter the hut and enjoy the tea. The guests once more view everything in the room: the new flower arrangement, the scroll, and the utensils. When they have quietly taken their seats, the host comes in and tells his guests that he will serve them tea. The guests watch the host rekindle the fire. Then they are served dry sweets. After that, the host cleanses the bowl in which he will serve the tea, the ceramic tea container, and bamboo scoop with his silk cloth. He then draws hot water from the kettle into the bowl and rinses the bamboo whisk. The water is emptied out, and the bowl wiped with a white, dampened linen cloth. As the host lifts the lid from the kettle, steam emerges, producing a sound that is often compared to the wind blowing through the pine trees, an image frequently employed by ancient Japanese poets. The host puts a measured amount of powdered tea into the bowl, adds some water, and kneads the still-compact tea. With a bit of more water, he blends the tea into the density he wants. The first tea is called *koicha*, or thick tea, and it is served in a single bowl that all guests must share. Each guest must leave enough tea in the bowl for the rest of the guests and must wipe off the spot of the bowl touched by his lips. After all have had their three sips and the bowl is now empty, the guests may request to see the tea container, its silk bag, and the tea scoop. As they are carefully inspecting these utensils, the host removes all other utensils from the room. He reenters the room after the last guest has viewed the utensils and has returned them to a predetermined spot near the host's seat. The main guest now asks the host: "What is the container's shape? Where was it made? Who carved the tea scoop? What name does it have?"

After this exchange, the host picks up these utensils and carries them out of the room, bowing to the guests from the door.

Soon the host reenters, carrying the utensils with which to prepare thin tea. The mood is now lighter and the host's movements quicker. He makes each guest a separate cup of tea. Heavy sweets are served before the host whisks the tea in the first bowl destined for the main guest. During this time, there may be some light conversation and the guests may request a closer examination of the thin tea container and tea scoop. After this, they will quietly view the alcove display and hearth once again and then leave. The host opens the guest entrance and makes a farewell bow to his guests, remaining in the doorway until they are out of sight. He sits for a moment reflecting upon the meeting, because it has been utterly unique and will never repeat itself. Finally, he cleanses the room and all the utensils. The room is now empty, all is as before, and it seems as if nothing has happened, except perhaps a quick stir on the surface of the water. [5]

Tea as Philosophy

T here is perhaps nothing more important for Hounsai than tea philosophy, and he is more aware of it and has written more about it than any of his predecessors. In the era of intense nationalism that ended in Japan's defeat in World War II, tea came to be considered innately and typically Japanese, and this view continues to this day among conservative tea devotees. Ever since 1906, when Okakura Tenshin (Kakuzo, 1862–1913) published his *Book of Tea* in New York, tea has provided Japan with a cultural identity that is clearly distinct from that of the West. It is easy for Japanese to ignore Chinese tea traditions because tea as a practice (way) has disappeared in modern China. In the postwar period of national redress and peace with neighboring nations Korea and China, Hounsai is perhaps the first tea master to acknowledge the debt that Japanese tea owes to China. In an effort to reintroduce tea to China, Hounsai sponsors the teaching of tea in Chinese universities. When Hounsai writes that "drinking a cup of tea means to immerse oneself in nature," he is in fact referring back to ancient Chinese Taoist philosophy.[1] The Chinese origins of tea are an essential aspect of tea that the Western reader who wishes to understand tea must grasp.

TAOISM

The origins of tea in China help explain why tea is not just a complicated way of quenching one's thirst but a way to restore health and to reestablish harmony between the individual and the universe. We can find the origin of Chinese ceremonial tea precisely in this holistic philosophy. This philosophy is eclectic, comprised of several systems of Chinese thought: (1) the identity of microcosms and macrocosms; (2) the Five Element theory and its correspondences; and (3) the yin-yang system and its classifications.

Chinese writings from the fifth century B.C.E. make it clear that the ancient Chinese understood the universe as an organic whole, each natural phenomenon owing its existence and its well-being to the rest of the universe in a complicated web of intrinsic interrelationships and codependences. In Taoism, the entire universe is regarded as one living organism; the microcosmic world is but a reflection of the macrocosmic one, and vice versa. Taoism stresses the inseparability of all things. Matter is not isolated from its environment. There is nothing in this universe, however different or remote, that does not influence all other things in the universe. The nature of a thing is only important and worth our attention when considered in its interrelatedness with other things—*Wechselbeziehung* in German. What happens to one thing necessarily affects the other; large things reflect the small and small things reflect the large.

The entire universe with all its infinite variety is contained in the human body. The head is like the heavens and the feet like the underworld. The deities who control the larger universe also reside in the various organs of the human body. The microcosm interacts constantly with the macrocosm. Health in the body and mind of individuals as well as the state depends on this interaction. According to this philosophy, the well-being of a nation and of its citizens hangs on their ability to maintain harmony among all their constituent elements, large and small. Loss of that harmony because of selfish, destructive behavior engenders disharmony and causes disease and destruction.

Taoist philosophers never clearly distinguished between body and soul, matter and spirit. Accordingly, harmony and well-being must be maintained by a body-soul, that is, a physical-spiritual unity and not by the body or mind as separate entities. This philosophy forms the way in which the Chinese continue to understand life. When a patient takes Chinese medicine or undergoes an acupuncture treatment, or drinks tea, a cure is effected by the restoration of harmony within his body-mind unity *cum* universe. At its inception, therefore, the drinking of tea involved not just the physical body, but also its spirit(s).[2]

This approach to physical and mental disease differs from the one we have developed in the West during the last three centuries. Earlier systems of Western thought, such as astrology and other occult sciences, more closely resemble the holistic approach of Taoism, and it is only since Descartes (1596–1650) that the West has subscribed to a philosophy based on the clear separation of matter and spirit. Modern Western science and medicine, with their analytic method of isolating elements and phenomena and the emphasis on treating organs in isolation and on surgery, are fundamentally different from Chinese medicine and science. Chinese medicine is not supposed to cure an individual organ but to restore the patient's harmony with the environment.

This holistic understanding of the mind-body unity developed in the various Taoist schools into a "science" of longevity and immortality. The Chinese belief in the possibility of achieving immortality in both body and mind differentiates it from the West. The Chinese "immortals" celebrated in Taoist folklore and the arts were believed to attain immortality in body and mind by controlling their body chemistry through severe austerities. Claiming that tea is a means to commune with the immortals, the *Isei Teikin Orai*, an anonymous fourteenth-century Japanese text that consists of questions and answers on tea, attests to the degree to which Japanese tea adopted this kind of thought: "The immortals sang in praise of tea, and humans, too, enjoyed it.... Tea promotes purity and humility and allows one to commune with the immortals."[3]

In order to achieve immortality, Chinese alchemists conducted studies and tests to find the elixir, the perfect chemistry, of eternal life. Hence the importance the Chinese have placed on longevity: the longer and better one lives, the closer one comes to attaining immortality. Chinese landscape painting, which, like tea, developed its basic styles during the Song dynasty (960–1279), often depicts places in nature considered particularly powerful, such as the confluence of rivers, or the emergence of rivers onto the plains, where Chinese immortals had allegedly attained their control over matter and spirit to become immortals.

Taoism also deeply affected traditional Chinese politics. For example, an emperor's poor administration was believed to have caused rivers to flood, crops to fail, and to throw the five seasons out of harmony. Winter music—for the Chinese categorized musical modes by season—played in the summer was believed to cause snowstorms.[4] Here we find the prime reason for one of the most basic rules of tea, which is to associate the tea utensils with the seasons as much as possible: for example, the use of thick tea bowls in the winter and thin, flat ones in the summer. Hounsai maintains that a tea without a specific seasonal reference is still strictly taboo.

The Chinese created a complex and all-encompassing classification system based on these basic Taoist beliefs. They divided the universe into Five Elements (wood, fire, water, metal, earth). In addition, all perceivable phenomena were given a male-female taxonomy, known as the yin-yang system. This classification derives from a holistic understanding of the universe and should be differentiated from superficially similar characteristics of Western culture, such as the masculine, feminine, and neutral articles of Indo-European languages. The Chinese used this system of yin-yang and the Five Elements for divination, but also in constituting the principles of government, court ceremonies, military science, medicine and pharmacology, and the arts. It became a system of reference to help people comprehend their universe, their lives, and the major events of their times. In his *Cha Jing* (The Book of Tea), Lu Yu (d. 804?), whom the Chinese revered as a god of tea, explicitly states, "When the Five Elements are in balance within the body, the Hundred Illnesses are expelled."[5] Hounsai understands this to mean that tea harmonizes the Five

Elements in the body, ensuring the body's health.[6] Health depends on the harmony and balance among all these elements.

According to the *Book of Changes* (*Yijing*, attributed to Confucius), yin and yang, female and male, emerged from the primordial chaos. Yang ascended to become heaven, whereas yin descended to become earth. Neither of these two elements can engender anything by itself; they can only procreate if they come together. It is out of their union that the many things in the world have come into being. When they come together, they engender such things as earth, mountains, water, wind, thunder, fire, marshes, and heaven. Yin and yang also subject the things they create to constant change, following certain measurable patterns that are predictable. For example, water gives birth to wood, wood gives birth to fire, fire gives birth to earth, earth gives birth to metal, and metal gives birth to water. At the same time, each element "overpowers" or "overcomes" another in the chain: water overcomes fire, fire overcomes metal, metal overcomes wood, wood overcomes earth, and earth overcomes water.[7]

There is no element that does not overcome the others in an eternal metamorphosis that is fixed and unchanging. These in turn drive other systems such as the Five Directions and the Five Human Relations and ultimately control the entire universe.

The Zen monk Eisai (also Yosai, 1141–1215) was fully aware of these basic precepts of Chinese philosophy when he introduced tea plants and the tea ritual to Japan at the end of the twelfth century. In 1187, Eisai traveled to China for the second time and stayed four years. When he returned to Japan in 1191, he brought with him tea seeds and enough knowledge about tea in China to establish it in Japan. Eisai's main motive in traveling to China and introducing Zen Buddhism and tea to Japan was to revitalize his declining country. Eisai wanted to restore Japan's spiritual and political harmony and unity after more than a century of war and social unrest. He traveled to China in an effort to find a new Buddhist teaching that would allow Japan to overcome the Buddhist apocalyptic age, supposed to have begun in the year 1052, one thousand five hundred years after the death of Gautama Buddha.

Eisai not only brought Zen Buddhism from China but also tea plants, knowledge about tea, and the Chinese philosophy of tea.[8] The Japanese had founded their state on Chinese models in the mid-seventh century. Through the centuries Japan continued to rely on China for political inspiration and as a model for revitalizing the nation in periods of decline. Eisai and his tea were therefore welcomed by other contemporary reformists such as the monk Myoe (1173–1232), who let Eisai grow the tea plants at his Kozanji temple in the Toganoo area of Kyoto, where one can see to this day Eisai's "original" tea plantation.

It is difficult for us now to understand how a cup of tea was supposed to transform a nation without understanding ideas about the cycle of loss and restoration of universal harmony current in China and Japan at this time — in other words, the ideas expressed in Taoist philosophy discussed above. Not coincidentally, Eisai introduced Taoist ideas when he presented his tea to the ruling shogun Minamoto no Sanetomo (1192–1219), the third shogun of the Kamakura period (1185–1333). Eisai had heard that the shogun drank too much and got sick during a banquet. He therefore decided to offer the shogun a bowl of tea that he brought with him from his temple, telling the shogun that it was good medicine. He also presented a booklet about the virtues of tea, which pleased the shogun greatly. This episode is recorded in the history entitled *Azuma Kagami* under the date February 3, 1214.[9]

Eisai had written this booklet, entitled *Kissa Yojo Ki* (Preservation of Health Through Drinking Tea) in an effort to help the shogun overcome the effects of drunkenness, but his goals for tea were more extensive, as we have seen: he wanted to employ tea to stop the political deterioration of his country and restore its harmony. In this booklet, Eisai associates tea with the Five Tastes: acid, pungent, bitter, sweet, and salty, which he correlated with six other groups of five:

1. the Five Organs: liver, lungs, heart, spleen, kidneys
2. the Five Sensory Organs: eyes, nose, tongue, mouth, ears
3. the Five Directions: east, west, south, center, north
4. the Five Planets: Jupiter, Venus, Mars, Saturn, Mercury
5. the Five Seasons: spring, autumn, summer, between-seasons (*doyo*),[10] winter
6. the Five Elements: wood, metal, fire, earth, water

Eisai related the Five Organs and the Five Tastes (food) in the following manner:

1. The liver likes sour taste.
2. The lungs like pungent taste.
3. The heart likes bitter taste.
4. The spleen likes sweet taste.
5. The kidneys like salty taste.

After clarifying these correspondences, Eisai applies the Five Organs to the Five Directions, the Five Seasons, the Five Elements, the Five Colors, the Five Spirits and the Five Sensory Organs:

> In addition, the Five Organs correspond to the Five Elements (wood, fire, earth, metal, water) and to the Five Directions (east, south, west, north, center). Consequently, the liver corresponds to east, spring, wood, blue, soul, and the eyes. The lungs correspond to west, fall, metal, white, the bodily soul, and the nose. The heart corresponds to south, summer, fire, red, deity, and tongue. The spleen corresponds to center, the end of the

four seasons, earth, yellow, will, and mouth. The kidneys correspond to north, winter, water, black, thought, bone marrow, and the ears.

These lists of mutual correspondences derive from the Taoist system of classification, as outlined above. Eisai explains what happens if the natural proportions of these correspondences are disrupted by excess.

> The tastes these organs like are all different. If a single organ receives an excess of its preferred taste, then it will grow strong at the expense of the other organs, causing them all to get sick. The four tastes—sour, pungent, sweet, and salty—are readily available, and we eat them often, but the bitter is not always available, and consequently we do not eat [enough] bitter food. Therefore, the four organs become stronger and stronger and the heart weaker and weaker and ultimately gets sick and, when the heart is sick, then all the tastes fall out of balance with each other and we vomit what we eat and whatever we do, we cannot eat anymore at all.

Through this pamphlet Eisai introduced the Taoist notion of universal balance to the shogun. He continues writing about the virtues of drinking bitter tea.

> If we drink tea, however, the heart is healthy and we avoid getting sick. Remember that when the heart is sick, one's skin assumes an unhealthy color and one dies young. Tastes are the same, whether one eats in Japan or abroad, but in Japan we do not eat bitter foods. Whereas the Chinese drink tea to provide the heart with the taste it likes, in Japan we do not drink tea. Therefore, the Chinese have healthy hearts and live long. This is why the Chinese are never thin. Conversely, in our country, many people have chronically sick hearts, the reason being that in our country people do not drink tea as in China. Therefore, when the Five Organs are out of harmony with each other and the heart is sick, one should drink tea. In so doing, the heart's condition improves and all illness disappears. When the heart is healthy, though the other organs may get sick, they do not get seriously sick.

If the heart is sick, he maintained, it needs bitter food to restore its health and harmony with the other organs, with the seasons, the directions, the planets, and the Five Elements controlling the universe.

Eisai continues by juxtaposing this system of quintuple elements with the Buddhas and bodhisattvas of Buddhism which, given the Buddhist-Taoist combination that had already developed in China, also played a role in his understanding and taxonomy of the universe. As one might expect, the central Buddha Mahavairocana (Jp. Dainichi) occupies the center together with the heart.

In the subsequent pages of his *Kissa Yojo Ki*, Eisai expands on tastes and sickness.

The heart is the chief of the Five Organs and the [bitter] taste of tea is the most important. In other words, bitter is the chief among the [Five] Tastes. This is why the heart likes bitter taste. It is healthy, thanks to the bitter foods it partakes, and secures the health of the other, subordinate organs. If one's eyes are sick, one's liver is bad and, since the liver likes sour food, one should take sour medicine. Also, if one's ears are sick, this is because the kidneys are bad and, since the kidneys like salty taste, one should take salty medicine to cure them.[11]

Eisai asserted that none of these elements is isolated from the others nor are they merely arbitrary systems of classification; he insists that they are truly and intimately related one to another. He correlated all these elements to the religious classification of the Five Buddhas, Five Symbols, Five Gestures (mudra), and Five Regions of the esoteric mandala. Like his Chinese predecessor Lu Yu, Eisai viewed tea as a good medicine for all ills, a panacea. He thus recommended that the shogun partake of the tea he had just brought back to Japan from his voyage to China.

Eisai's tea spread first through the Zen temples he founded (especially his first temple, Kenninji in Kyoto, founded in 1202). Afterward it was transmitted through the shoguns and merchants of the Ashikaga period (1336–1573), and from generation to generation of tea people down to Sen Rikyu. Through Rikyu, it was passed down to later tea masters, including Hounsai. Let us look at the way this Chinese philosophy helped create the tea we know today.

Rikyu saw the shape of the sixteenth-century tea hut and tea room as a model of yin-yang and therefore as a miniature model of the universe. The earliest theoretical treatises on this subject, however, postdate his death in 1591. We can infer from the following quotation from the *Nanboroku*, a book on Rikyu's tea published at the one-hundredth anniversary of Rikyu's death and allegedly authored by Rikyu's disciple Nanbo Sokei (dates unknown), that Rikyu's tea was influenced by the belief in a correspondence between the tea room and the universe: "Guest and host are yin-yang, water and fire are also yin-yang . . . you cannot divorce yin and yang from the rules governing the grass-thatched [tea] hut; they complement each other."[12]

Sokei provides specific guidelines for implementing this theoretical scheme by explaining that the host should always draw the water at dawn regardless of when in the day he plans on serving tea.

> Regardless of whether the [tea] gathering takes place in the morning, noon, or at night, one must draw the water at dawn. This is the rule of tea. One must draw enough water to last from dawn till evening. A night tea service is no excuse for drawing the water in the afternoon. From evening till midnight, yin reigns; the water spirits sink and poison prevails. Dawn, the time one draws the water, is the beginning of yang, when the pure spirits

emerge. Dawn water is the flower of the well and, being vital for tea, it requires special care on the part of the host.[13]

There is no doubt that Rikyu abided by this rule and made sure his disciples would do the same. Dawn water is yang and corresponds to the zodiac sign of the Tiger, representing the beginning of the year and of the day. The water thus drawn is fresh, new water, the water of yang, the first element that came into existence in the universe.

When it comes to the display of tea utensils in the tea room, Rikyu tells us through the "Metsugo" (Posthumous) section of the *Nanboroku*, students need many years of practice to determine what is yin and what is yang: "From the hundred, thousand, even ten thousand ways to display utensils on the *daisu* table, everything has to accord with yin and yang, and one needs many years of practice to master it all."[14]

These three quotations demonstrate that Rikyu understood tea as ritual precisely because it harmonizes these structural elements of the universe. Tea recreates the universe in miniature.

Rikyu's descendents continued to apply the yin-yang system to their tea. Eleventh-generation Urasenke grand tea master Gengensai (1810–77) wrote about this in his *Gengensai Chado Sosho*: "Originally, the four-and-a-half mat room was modeled on the yin-yang and Five Elements, containing the entire universe in a single room. People claim that this came from Zen but, in fact, it originated in the *Book of Changes* and the *Book of Rites*."[15] Gengensai understood the system to have derived from Confucianism rather than Taoism because, in his time, Taoism had ceased to exist in Japan as a separate philosophical system. Over the centuries, Confucianism had become the official philosophy of the government, but it was a Confucianism that had long ago ingested the main ideas of Taoism.

It is because of the yin-yang system that, according to Gengensai, the host should face north when preparing tea. The four sides of the tea room with winter in the north represent the four seasons, and doyo, the fifth season, is in the middle. He was following Rikyu, whose tea hut Yamazato, which he designed for the warlord Toyotomi Hideyoshi (1536–98) in 1584, faced north.

Gengensai also developed the *gogyodana* (table of the Five Elements) as a miniature universe. It epitomizes the relation of tea with the Five Elements. The top shelf (*ten ita*) represents heaven (yang) and the bottom shelf (*ji ita*), earth (yin). Three bamboo posts support heaven. The fire and metal kettle filled with water are placed between heaven and earth. In their ensemble, the brazier made of earth, and the fire, the kettle, and the water it contains represent the creative forces of heaven and earth.[16]

In many of his writings and speeches, Hounsai echoes his predecessors, explaining how this yin-yang system shaped the tea procedures as well as the orientation of the tea rooms, tea huts, and even the location of utensils. The manner of preparing tea using fire to boil water in a metal kettle and scooping it with a bamboo (wooden) ladle into an earthen tea bowl is a way of harmonizing the Five Elements and recreating the microcosm. According to Hounsai, the four-and-one-half mat tea room—which became standard in the sixteenth century under Rikyu—represents the four seasons, and the half-mat, the in-between seasons (doyo).[17] Similarly, the *fukusa* silk cloth that the host uses to cleanse the tea utensils has a yin and a yang side. When it is tucked in one's belt, the outer side represents heaven, or yang, and the inner side earth, or yin. When one folds the cloth into fourths, it comes to represent the Four Directions. When one purifies tea utensils with the silk cloth, one also purifies, by extension, the Four Directions. "Tea represents the entire universe," he wrote.[18] Like Eisai, Hounsai combines Taoism and Buddhism: the four corners represent the Four Heavenly Kings who protect the realm of the Buddhas from all evil, and when the cloth is folded into eighths, beyond which one can no longer fold it, one enters into the realm of Buddhist enlightenment.[19]

Hounsai also interprets the opposites in tea as a balance of yin and yang: "Tea rejoices in opposites. Balance between disparate elements is continuously sought. Where fire is used, water will also be found. . . . The round will be balanced with the square, the heavy with the light. . . . Sound and the absence of sound during a tea gathering also illustrate this principle." [20] Emphasizing the balance of opposites and extremes, Hounsai keeps himself within the Taoist tradition.

ZEN BUDDHISM

At the time of Eisai's visit to China, the holistic philosophy of Taoism had already merged considerably with Zen Buddhist thought. After all, Eisai was a Buddhist monk who is revered as the first to introduce Zen Buddhism to Japan. His strong interest in Taoism evident in the *Kissa Yojo Ki* is testimony to the blending of the two traditions that had already taken place in China. After Eisai, however, Japanese tea devotees shifted the emphasis from Taoism to "purer" Zen philosophy. During Rikyu's time, tea practitioners were strongly conscious of the relationship between tea and Zen. As Yamanoue Soji (1544–90), one of Rikyu's disciples, pointed out: "Tea originated in Zen, therefore [Zen] monks transmitted it." [21] Although allegedly trained by the monk Ikkyu Sojun (1394–1481) of the temple Daitokuji, Murata Juko (1423–1502) failed to elaborate specifically on Zen and tea. It was not until the publication in the Tokugawa period (1600–1868) of the *Nanboroku* that an elaborate discussion of the relationship between Zen and tea appeared.

Buddhism is the earliest of the world's great soteriological religions, preceding Christianity by about half a millennium and Islam by over a millennium. Born as a north-Indian royal prince, the Buddha (a title meaning the Enlightened One, given to him later by his disciples) had taught that self-discipline leads to enlightenment. Enlightenment allows one to escape the suffering of life. Buddhism sees all forms of temporary worldly existence as suffering. The Buddhist ideal is to escape from the endless round of rebirths by seeking nirvana (cessation) through enlightenment, thus avoiding reincarnation. As one of many Buddhist teachings, Zen emphasized imitating the lifestyle and self-discipline of the Buddha as the best way to attain enlightenment, or in other words, Buddhahood. Zen follows Mahayana Buddhism in its belief that all living things carry in themselves the seeds for enlightenment. A well-known Zen parable Hounsai likes to quote says that "People are divided into north and south, but Buddhahood knows of no north nor south." Mahayana Buddhism teaches that the avenue towards Buddhahood differs with each individual, hence the Zen emphasis on discovering oneself through means suited to the individual seeker. This is why Hounsai encourages the cultivation of one's heart as tea's ultimate aim; salvation comes through introspection, looking inside rather than outside of oneself. Zen monks and tea people often represent this idea in paintings portraying two seventh-century Chinese monks, Hanshan and Shihde (Kanzan and Jittoku in Japanese). Each was enlightened by following his own, proper calling; one by sweeping the floor and the other by reading a book. Kanzan-Jittoku paintings are often displayed at tea meetings to send out the message that tea, too, is a form of self-discipline and a way toward self-discovery.

Many tea devotees understood tea as a form of Buddhist discipline and a way toward enlightenment. According to the *Nanboroku* and the *Zencharoku* (Zen Tea Record), attributed to the Zen monk Jakuan Sotaku and published in 1828 in Edo, the fathers of tea such as Murata Juko, Sen Rikyu, and Sen Sotan always took enlightenment as the ultimate aim of their art. Based on passages in the "Oboegaki" (Memoranda) section of the *Nanboroku*, for example, we can surmise that Rikyu saw tea as Buddhist practice. To the question, "Why is it that the informal tea held in a small room is best to attain the deepest meaning of tea?" Rikyu allegedly replied:

> Tea of the small room is most importantly a place to practice Buddhist discipline. Indulging in the luxuries of home and savoring culinary delicacies are things that belong to the [mundane] world [and have no place in tea]. A house is enough when it does not leak, a meal is enough when one does not starve. This is the teaching of the Buddha and the essence of tea. I draw water, gather firewood, boil water, and make tea. I [then] offer some to the Buddha and some to my guests and reserve some for myself. I arrange flowers and burn incense. I do all of this as Buddhist training.[22]

For Rikyu, tea and Buddhism were inseparable. In his speeches and writings, Hounsai tries to keep this teaching alive as one of the most fundamental in tea. "Tea of the small room" is another way of saying *wabi* (frugal, poor) tea, in contrast to the more elaborate and yet mundane *shoin* (reception-room) tea. In the small room, tea is reduced to a simple ritual of offering a cup to the Buddha and then to the guests. Nothing artificial may interrupt or draw attention away from the essentials, which are boiling water and making tea in a hut that does not leak and serving just enough food to prevent starvation. It became customary to discuss tea in terms of Zen after the *Nanboroku* was written. This was perhaps an attempt to legitimize tea as a serious religious practice that would improve the behavior of leaders and subjects. One of the most thorough and deepest discussions of Zen tea, however, is found in the *Zencharoku*. Because later tea people quoted from it often, we know that this work was read as a kind of spiritual guide. Since the views of the *Zencharoku* correspond to those of Hounsai, it is worthwhile to pay attention to its main points, especially because the *Zencharoku* is, in the opinion of this author, one of the best sources for understanding Zen Buddhism.

The author of the *Zencharoku*, Jakuan Sotaku, severely criticizes contemporary tea's ignorance of Zen and its emphasis on correct procedure without regard for Buddhist practice and discipline. "Practicing tea in any other way than to find the true essence of things is like a blind man cracking his head with his own fist," maintains Jakuan.[23] Jakuan was a fundamentalist who regretted tea's secularization and spiritual degeneracy. He wanted to return tea to its religious origin, to inspire a spiritual renaissance, as Eisai had done in the twelfth century. The "Metsugo" section of the *Nanboroku* had already warned that ten years after Rikyu tea would die out, though, ironically, people would think that it flourishes. Jakuan argued that form should not be allowed to exist only for form's sake. One should always seek substance behind form and formality; only then does tea have meaning, declared Jakuan.

Jakuan tried to take tea back to the golden age when the monk Ikkyu Sojun first established the Zen-tea combination. "Tea and the Way of Buddha are the same," wrote Ikkyu, "and, when serving tea, the spirit of Zen appears as a way to demonstrate one's heart to the public; therefore, whenever one serves tea, there is the Way of Zen."[24] He also wrote, "The meaning of tea is the meaning of Zen. Therefore, if one abandons the meaning of Zen, then there can no longer be a meaning of tea. If one does not know the meaning of Zen, one cannot know the meaning of tea."[25]

These statements are a polemic aimed at rescuing tea from a mundane form of entertainment and restoring it to Zen practice and philosophy. Jakuan wanted to remove tea from a culture that emphasized social distinctions and elaborate entertainment, and return it to the very foundation of Buddhist philosophy. "Therefore," he writes, "to indulge in luxuries, to always drink the best wine, or to build elaborate tea rooms and play with [the shapes of] garden trees and rocks is contrary to the original meaning of tea. The essence of tea is to earnestly practice Zen tea. Serving tea is nothing but Zen, a way to discover ones original Buddhahood."

For Jakuan, the practice of tea is the same as the Buddhist notion of *samadhi* (right perception), which means to fix one's mind immovably on a single point and is one of the principal precepts of Zen meditation. He maintains that zazen (seated meditation) is none other than samadhi. Depending on one's frame of mind the practice of zazen is comparable to tea. Jakuan reverses the maxim "tea is Zen" by saying that "Zen is tea."

Zen tea should be an expression of a selfless self; it should communicate at the minimal level of essences. From this point of view, attachment to formalities is particularly reprehensible. Jakuan maintains that tea is not appreciating utensils or scrutinizing the circumstances and arrangements of a tea gathering, but is solely religious praxis: "The utensils of Zen tea are not beautiful utensils, they are not treasures, they are not antiques, they are merely objects revealing one's pure and undefiled heart. If they are the receptacles of a pure heart, then it is tea in the true sense of Zen."[26]

For him the famous utensils (*meibutsu*) that occupied center stage in tea are unworthy of our attention. Strange and unusual tea bowls are simply old crockery and antique heirlooms. They seem to enlarge our existence, but they are nothing more than reflections of our imagined selves and are contrary to Buddhist ideals. Utensils should be as "empty of self" as the host using them, manifesting a unity of spirit between host and his utensils. Tea, like Zen, should obliterate the distinctions between subject and object. Zen practitioners perceive no beings or things separate from themselves, no self apart from things. When subjectivity is eliminated, the world and things appear as they truly are, which is the Buddhist notion of "such-ness" (*tathata*). Self-interest blinds one from this realization.

The *Zencharoku* warned people of the evil inclinations of egocentrism, which turn tea into a social ritual or an extravagant display.

> When one stirs up one's heart by what one thinks is wabi, extravagance is born; When one stirs up one's heart by utensils, it leads to measurements; When one stirs up one's heart by what one thinks is *suki* (refinement), *konomi* [preferred style] is born; When one stirs up one's heart by what one thinks is nature, artifice is born; When one stirs up one's heart by what one considers sufficient, insufficiency is born; When one stirs up one's heart thinking that it is the Way of Zen, heresy is created. When one stirs oneself up by such [illusory] thoughts, all leads to evil inclinations.[27]

Jakuan argues that one must practice tea in a selfless (muga) state and that self-consciousness is self-defeating. Referring to the tea path (roji), Jakuan argues that it is more than a mere path, it is an avenue toward enlightenment. Tea should be a way of life so that one is left with no regrets at the end of one's life: "The day will come when one will be reborn in the Pure Land of Buddha. Therefore we must

heed the warnings of the suki [amateurs] and solely practice Zen tea to gain enlightenment. When one attains the realm of no-birth, no-death, then what regret may
one have left when one faces death?" [28]

Even the Europeans, who had discovered Japan in 1542, noticed how closely tea
was linked to Zen. João Rodrigues (1561–1634) was one among many European missionaries and merchants to report on Japanese tea. Because of tea's religious neu-
trality, early Catholic missionaries not only observed tea as a non-Christian practice,
but actually adopted the art in their own Church curriculum. For Rodrigues, the
Portuguese interpreter, tea represented the best in the Japanese character: "The
Japanese have come to detest any contrivance and elegance, any pretense,
hypocrisy, or outward embellishment. Their ideal is to promise little but accomplish
much, to use moderation in everything, and to desire to err by default rather than by
excess." [29] What Rodrigues thus attributed to the Japanese character, was nothing
but Zen tea in practice.

As the present grand master of the Urasenke school of tea, Hounsai inherited the
Zen of Eisai, Juko, and Rikyu, as well as the Zen of the *Nanboroku* and the
Zencharoku. He understands tea as essentially Zen practice. Having himself undergone rigorous Zen training at the temple Daitokuji in Kyoto, he rarely fails to bring
together tea and Zen in his speeches and writings. In his *Reflections on Chanoyu*
he wrote:

> Within traditional culture, tea possesses qualities that set it apart from the
> other arts. In the Noh and Kabuki theaters, for example, the focus is on a
> stage, and performers and audiences face each other from different posi-
> tions. In tea this is not the case, inasmuch as host and guests occupy the
> same places. . . . The tea room is a real-life setting for the important prac-
> tice in the Way of Zen of seeking oneness of host and guests. [30]

Here, Hounsai points out the need in Zen to abolish all distinctions that
separate and isolate things and people. In another of his many books, Hounsai
discusses the Zen teaching of finding enlightenment in an emptied mind:

> The Rinzai sect of Zen [founded by Eisai] says that we should be centered
> so that wherever we are, whatever happens, we never lose the infantile, pri-
> mal mind we are born with. The primal mind is the same as Zen's no-mind
> or emptiness of mind. If we are one with it we can overcome our self-
> consciousness and attachments. In order for us to reach this state, we need
> a discipline or way along which to travel in search of our primal mind. [31]

Overcoming our self-consciousness and attachments means overcoming all distinctions that separate us from each other and which, in tea, separate host and guest.
This is the meaning behind Chinese Zen master Zhaozhou Wuzi's (1183–1260)

parable *"Muhinshu"* (No Host, No Guest). *"Honrai Muichibutsu"* (Originally All Is One and Undifferentiated), which the Chinese monk Taman Hungjen (d. 675) told his disciples when he was close to attaining enlightenment, is one of Hounsai's favorite Zen parables. [32] (See page 32 for a more detailed discussion of these parables.)

Hounsai has always stressed the links between Zen and tea. For him, everything applicable to Zen is also applicable to tea, and vice versa. Tea is a discipline to free our minds from the constructs of civilization, a discipline that enables us to purify the senses and the mind from egocentrism. Tea procedures are therefore not the end but, as he wrote in spring 1970, "a means and process and . . . a necessary condition for the activity of the spirit. . . . tea must transcend its own form." [33]

Hounsai therefore dislikes tea meetings focusing on little more than the display of rare and expensive utensils. In an interview of August 9, 1998, Hounsai pointed out to me that utensils are used in tea to unite, not separate, host and guest. Also, he insisted, the tea room is a space for achieving unity in diversity, a place to unite individuals, not to separate them by emphasizing social and economic distinctions. To unite people, one must first reach a compromise. One must be able to compromise the self or, in Buddhist terms, create a selfless *mu* mind that overcomes the separation of self and other.

Hounsai takes the tea-Zen combination even further. He understands tea as involving all of our sensory organs: eyes, ears, nose, tongue, body, and mind. [34] The various sounds the host produces while making tea should all be as natural as possible. The water being poured into the tea bowl with a bamboo ladle suggests water running from a bamboo pipe. The whisk produces the sound of a mountain stream. As we have seen earlier, the sound of the steam emerging from the kettle is often described as resembling the wind blowing through the pine trees. For Hounsai, these sounds do not disturb the tranquility of the tea hut, they enhance it. Then there is the paradoxical Zen of "hearing" rather than smelling incense, as practiced in the *kagetsu* (flower and moon) tea ritual. This creates a kind of multisensory experience. It is like hearing or smelling a painting. In the following poem, Sotan expressed the effect tea can have on the senses:

> *When someone asks you:*
> *What is the nature of tea?*
> *Say it's the sound*
> *Of the wind blowing through the pines*
> *In a painting.*

To be able to answer thus, however, the senses must be disciplined. Tea provides an ideal environment for cultivating the discipline of multisensory aesthetic experience. Emphasizing the efficacy of Zen practice to unite one's senses, Hounsai describes the heightened sensory awareness that tea can produce: "In the microcosm of the tea room . . . the boundaries of the senses blur and sensations tend to run, like liquids, into each other; vision assumes a tactile character, touch and sound suggest visual images."[35] Many Zen monks have reported similar experiences of crossing over sensory boundaries during long hours of meditation. In her *Chanoyu Kanwa* (Quiet Talk on Tea), Hamamoto Soshun, one of Hounsai's tea teachers, sums up this experience in the following manner: "True practice of tea brings all the six senses to function simultaneously and in accord, and leads to the realm of immovable tranquility."[36]

Ichigo ichie (one time, one meeting) is one of the tea teachings inspired by Zen. It was the daimyo Ii Naosuke (1815–60) who, in his work entitled *Chanoyu Ichie Shu*, stressed this principle in tea for the first time. Ever since, tea masters have tried to integrate this principle into their tea. In the manner in which Hounsai emphasizes this philosophy, we realize how profoundly Hounsai's tea is inspired by Zen. According to Hounsai, ichigo ichie brings tea and Zen together. "Ichigo ichie," he writes, "does not simply refer to a chance or good opportunity, or to a mere momentary coming together of things. It implies an infinitely more subtle concept."

After having thus warned his readers of what ichigo ichie is not, Hounsai continues:

> In terms of tea, ichigo ichie is manifest in the profound communion that comes about when host welcomes guest and guest sits together with host, with a bowl of tea as the mediating element. The host makes an offering of a bowl of tea to the guest; the guest partakes of and savors the offering. Through this very natural gesture, there arises a deep communion between the two. The delicate stirring of the soul; the quiet, lingering charm and sweet pathos aroused when host and guest share such a moment together—these things, the true essence of which can never be expressed in words, leave a distinct and memorable impression in the depths of the heart. It is this, combined with the realization that within a lifetime one may never again have the opportunity to steep oneself in such a fulfilling experience, that is the manifestation of ichigo ichie.

Ichigo ichie forces the host to do his utmost to make the meeting unique and memorable. This kind of merging of host and guest produces a deep communion and kindred spirit, similar to that achieved by people sitting in Zen meditation together. This derives from the Zen teachings on mutual enlightenment, whereby each person contributes to the enlightenment of the other.

Reflecting upon the events of that brief time spent together during the tea gathering, a certain emotion is aroused—the emotion or impression that those events have been etched on one's heart. When host and guest are able to share a moment in perfect spiritual harmony, the host giving of himself to the fullest, and the guests reciprocating, a cherished impression will live on in each of their hearts. These things do not come about by chance or accident. They are made possible through the host's careful preparations and attention to every detail of the gathering, and the guests' wholehearted appreciation of all that he has provided. Such a tea experience manifests the essence of "one time, one meeting." [37]

Tea as an Aesthetic

Aesthetics are an essential feature of all rituals. Many cultures believe that the deities themselves taught mankind their ritual arts, not only as the way for the gods to express themselves to mankind but also as the sole way humanity can communicate with the gods. The pictorial arts, literature, dance, and song started as ritual and only gradually became secularized—that is, like tea, turned into an expression of relations not between god and man but of man and man. All ritual has a social dimension, and the aim of ritual aesthetics is to unite a people in all their diversity, creating unity and harmony within diversity through participation in a common culture. This definition of ritual arts fits tea so well that it is difficult to consider tea as anything else but a ritual art. Social harmony through ritual and art is indeed what tea is all about.

Aiming at social harmony, tea has developed two important aesthetic traditions. One is the wabi aesthetic of minimal beauty, and the other is the luxurious and elaborate shoin aesthetic as an expression of social hierarchy. Chronologically, the shoin aesthetic precedes the wabi aesthetic. It appears that the wabi aesthetic is a reaction against the shoin aesthetic, but this distinction fails to account for the different sociopolitical conditions that engendered these two styles of tea. The shoguns of the Ashikaga family developed shoin tea as a ritual display of wealth and power in the fifteenth century, when the nation was relatively stable. Wabi tea, however, which seeks harmony by creating social equality, began in the Warring States Period (1467–1568) as a reaction against social and political instability and war. The shoin aesthetic ritually confirms the existing social order, whereas the wabi aesthetic drew its ideas of social leveling and equality from Japanese renewal rituals. Wabi tea, which emphasizes non-differentiation, appears more spiritual than shoin tea. Let us now expand more on the meaning of the wabi and shoin aesthetics and the arts they engendered.

31

Wabi tea creates a simple, unpretentious beauty that is easy for all participants to identify with. It contrasts with the ostentatious, opulent beauty that the wealthy and powerful seek to display in order to impress and intimidate. Like the stone gardens of the Ryoanji and other Zen temples in Kyoto, wabi tea eschews variety for a radical reduction to some fundamental, utterly simple element. It suggests a basic unity and simplicity underlying all things that is shared by rich or poor.

What is more, wabi tea encourages spiritual humility, a negation of the self and subsequent absorption in something larger. This humility is expressed in the Buddhist notion of "*Muichibutsu*" (Not One Thing Left), the emptiness of nonbeing. Hounsai often reminds his guests of this principle when displaying a scroll with the calligraphy "*Honrai Muichibutsu*" (Originally All Is One and Undifferentiated) to welcome his guests.

> On several occasions when I have written "*Honrai Muichibutsu*," I have been concerned that the people who see the calligraphy might feel that the phrase suggests poverty or want, and be touched in an unpleasant way. For me, this interpretation could not be further from the true meaning of the phrase. "*Honrai Muichibutsu*," on the contrary, is an affirmation of the positive and vital aspects of all that is; that the world, as it is, is sufficient.[1]

Another Zen expression Hounsai likes is "*Muhinshu*," meaning that there is no difference between host and guest. Social discrimination has no place in wabi tea; all become equal. There is a story of a tea party to which Rikyu invited a merchant as the main guest. While the gathering was in progress, a powerful lord visited Rikyu on business and requested to be admitted to the gathering. Rikyu agreed on the condition that the merchant, despite his low social status, continue as main guest and that the lord should take the last seat. The lord participated congenially, without ill feelings. Despite his social position and power, he accepted tea as a unique locus of fundamental human equality.

The *Zencharoku*, perhaps the most complete and elaborate source on the wabi aesthetic, explains the concept in terms of Zen Buddhism:

> Whatever one may say, wabi means deprivation without being conscious of being deprived. . . . The meaning of wabi . . . is limitation, but one does not conceive it as a lack of freedom. Similarly, insufficiency is not conceived of as insufficiency and the irregularity is not conceived of as irregularity. This is what wabi is. When one thinks of limitation as a lack of freedom and regrets insufficiency as insufficiency and accuses the irregular as not being regular, this is not wabi, but is [the thought of] a real beggar.[2]

Of course, this "deprivation" is to be taken positively, not as utter frustration and attachment to things but as a kind of Buddhist liberation from all attachments and desires. It comes from the Buddhist teaching of attaining contentment through having few desires, or from the definition the Buddha gave to the notion of contentment: "Feeling no regret at having little." It is the contentment we feel when we are satisfied to possess less: "Limit your desires and be content with little. What difference is there [between much and little]? The Buddha said: 'The one who desires little, seeks little and takes little. The one who knows how much is enough, gets little without regret.'" [3]

Wabi invites such a positive attitude—an inner satisfaction with the fact that one has barely enough to survive. Wabi, therefore, is not seeking poverty so much as it is a spiritual liberation from oppressive materialism. Jakuan understood wabi not so much as an aesthetic ideal but as an expression of a selfless poverty and the Buddhist teaching of emptiness (*sunyata*). Poverty is defined as the self freed from self-attachment and aware of its own finitude. This is the self in tune with what is real and timeless. This reminds one of the *Nanboroku*'s definition of wabi as being outside the human world, a place where one can wipe off the dust of the mundane and enter the "empty" world of the Buddha.

Zen Buddhism provided the spiritual foundation for wabi. Many tea masters, including Hounsai, studied and practiced Zen. Murata Juko allegedly studied under Ikkyu Sojun; Takeno Jo'o, a Sakai leather merchant, studied under the Zen monk Kogaku Soko; and Dairin Soto and Rikyu studied under Shorei Sokin, all monks from the Kyoto temple Daitokuji. These early tea masters all agree on one principle: in order to achieve wabi, one must practice Zen. In the spirit of Zen, the pursuit of wabi must be natural and unconstrained. Jo'o warned in his *Jo'o's Instructions for his Disciples*: "When one struggles to create beauty, it becomes a superficial decor. Likewise, when one strives for wabi, it becomes unsightly, and both turn into a fake. You must take special care [not to fall into this trap]." [4] Wabi, for Jo'o, must be a natural outcome of Buddhist training.

We can discover wabi in the simplicity of the Yuin tea room at Urasenke, and in some of the tea bowls the Korean potter Raku Chojiro (dates unknown) made for Sen Rikyu. We can discover it in Takeno Jo'o's preference for everyday objects— ordinary kitchen utensils, for example. Murata Juko, Takeno Jo'o's predecessor, expressed wabi with the image of "a precious horse tied to a shabby hut." [5] The contrast of wealth (the precious horse) and poverty (the shabby hut) in close proximity suggests something deeply spiritual and mysterious, something beyond mere appearances; it stimulates our aesthetic awareness and imagination and makes us concentrate on what cannot be seen. This is what wabi in tea is all about. The use of a famous tea utensil in a poor wabi hut would have the same effect.

Tea masters repeatedly associated the term wabi with imperfect, irregular beauty. Alluding to the *Essays in Idleness* (*Tsurezuregusa*, ca. 1340) by Urabe Kenko (1283–1350), Murata Juko wrote, "The moon is not pleasing unless partly clouded." [6]

A bright, full moon is not as pleasing as one that is partially obscured by a roof, clouds, tree branches, or other natural objects. Imperfection forces the mind to perfect the sight by involving the viewer more deeply in it. In the process, the sight becomes more spiritual. Kenko elaborated this point in his *Essays in Idleness*:

> Should we to look at the cherry blossoms only when they are in full bloom, and at the moon only when it shines clearly? It moves us more deeply to long for the moon while it rains or to lower the blinds and let spring pass by unawares.... After having waited for it all night long, the moon that appears close to dawn moves us more profoundly than the one that shines unobstructed over a thousand leagues.[7]

The combination of the impermanent, changing, yet somewhat predictable moon behind unpredictable and shifting clouds makes the sight beautiful and moving. The mind is encouraged to imagine what is hidden—the moon shining in a cloudless sky—without actually seeking it in this perfect state. The cherry blossoms, too, seem more beautiful before they bloom or after they have scattered for the same reason: the mind is stimulated to imagine how they will look or did look at their height.

Tea masters of the past have applied this principle to damaged tea utensils. A damaged utensil invites one to imagine its beauty when it was new, and it is this act of imagination that renders the object even more beautiful. The "Oboegaki" section of the *Nanboroku*, for example, severely criticizes those who only consider undamaged utensils worthy of use and display: "In the small room, one should keep the utensils at a minimum. There are people who dislike utensils with the slightest defect, which indicates that they do not understand at all."[8]

Rikyu's tea bowl named "Onjoji" was prized precisely because it cracked, and the tea bowl "Seppo" (Snowy Peak) belonging to the artist Hon'ami Koetsu (1558–1637) was valued because it had been repaired. The many cracks and the irregular shape of the "Yaburebukuro" (Bursting Bag) jar of the Iga kiln are what make it interesting. The same applies to the *kutsugata* (shoe-shaped) tea bowls Rikyu's disciple Furuta Oribe liked so much, and which Hounsai uses so often.

Before it became an aesthetic norm of tea, linked-verse (*renga*) poets used wabi as a guiding principle of poetry, often referring to two exemplary poems, one by Fujiwara Teika (1162–1241) and the other by Fujiwara Ietaka (1158–1237). Teika's poem reads as follows:

> *I look out far,*
> *And see neither*
> *Blossoms nor crimson leaves,*
> *But only a poor fisherman's hut*
> *At the head of the bay*[9]

The blossoms and crimson leaves represent the colors sought by the nobles of the capital Kyoto; tea people interpreted it to represent the splendor of shoin tea. But now that the urban splendor of the capital had waned, there was only the desolate world of the provinces, or the bleak world of wabi. This poem, composed at Futamigaura Bay near Ise, seems to express the feelings shared by many nobles who, like Teika, lamented the decline of the capital and its culture. It introduces into court culture the dark, monochrome vision of wabi. According to the *Nanboroku*, Jo'o claimed that the poem expresses the state of *"Muichibutsu"* that Teika had reached when contemplating the hut, and he compared the blossoms and crimson leaves to the beauty of shoin tea.

The *Nanboroku* quotes Rikyu as saying the following about these poems: "People in the mundane world wait all day long outside wondering when the cherry trees will bloom on this mountain or in that forest, and they do not realize that [Teika's] blossoms and crimson leaves were [only] in his heart; they only delight in the colors of what they see in front of their eyes."[10] Rikyu tried to integrate the same "heart" into tea. For him, the fisherman's hut was the essence of wabi. The experience of wabi is achieved by applying the human heart to things, to see things through the emotions that the merging of heart and object produces.

Rikyu liked to quote Teika's poem in tandem with the following poem by Fujiwara Ietaka:

> For those who only wait
> To see the blossoms,
> I wish I could show
> A spring of grass amid the snow
> In a mountain village.[11]

Rikyu discovered in this poem the true spirit of wabi: "Spring has come and, facing the sun, green grasses somehow emerge from between the patches of snow, like one or two leaves [from a tree branch]. The poet took this as the essence of what is true and unconstrained."[12] These were the two poems Jo'o and Rikyu integrated into the Way of Tea as true examples of how tea should be.

With its emphasis on the aesthetic concept of *yugen*, or mysterious depth, the Noh drama also contributed to the wabi tradition. The celebrated playwrights Kan'ami (Kanze Kiyotsugu, 1333–84) and his son Zeami (1363–1443) tried to present a deeper, more mysterious world than the one offered by the action of the play. The extreme restraint of the Noh performance style recalls both the stone garden of the temple Ryoanji and the strict economy of movement in Rikyu's tea. Poetry, Noh, and tea all participated in a common culture that grew out of the middle ages.

The possibility that wabi culture may have derived from Song-dynasty China, the same dynasty that created Japanese tea, is still debated among Japanese tea experts. The paintings of Mu Ji and Yu Qien, for example, exhibit the same principles and worldview as the wabi aesthetic. The suppression and abbreviation of expression we find in the works of these painters seem to indicate that wabi is an East Asian rather than exclusively Japanese cultural trait. Song painters chose monochrome techniques to enhance a subjective expression of ideas and images. They minimized objective representation in favor of creating, like Teika's *ushin* ("with heart," a principle of Japanese poetics), Noh, and tea, a world much deeper and more resonant than the surface of appearances.

Rikyu's sons Doan and Shoan and his grandson Sotan continued the wabi tradition. Sotan's two-mat tea room Konnichian, built in 1646, is an expression of his grasp of wabi. The room is just big enough to serve tea to one guest, creating an atmosphere of extreme closeness and intimacy between host and guest. Heir to this tradition, Hounsai particularly likes Okakura Tenshin's definition of wabi and often quotes it when he is explaining tea to non-Japanese. "[Teaism] is a cult founded on the adoration of the beautiful among the sordid facts of everyday existence. . . . It is essentially a worship of the Imperfect, as it is a tender attempt to accomplish something possible in this impossible thing we know as life."[13] Hounsai wrote that he would have preferred "the appreciation of" rather than "a worship of," but nevertheless, "I think Okakura's statement gives us a wonderfully poetic insight into the nature of the aesthetic of wabi."[14]

According to Hounsai, tea must not become a synonym of wabi but an inevitable facet, a natural result of wabi. Speaking about the *kannazuki* ("month of no gods"), an old name for November, he writes, "The month of no gods, as well as evening, are the times that tend to put us in a rather forlorn and dismal mood, and indeed these sorts of emotions are pivotal elements in the aesthetic of wabi. . . . there is a beauty of high order to be discovered in this seeming wretchedness; a beauty that is all the more exquisite precisely because we discover in it the wretched and the imperfect."[15]

Hounsai explains this in terms of the Zen teachings he has learned from his predecessors and from the monks of the temple Daitokuji: "Thus, the negative always embodies the positive; the imperfect always embodies the perfect. By realizing this, we can enjoy a beauty of a most exquisite kind even among the sordid facts of everyday existence."[16]

Hounsai likes to use wabi-style tea utensils: bucket-shaped water containers (*mizusashi*), simple bamboo vases, or flowers arranged in a leaking, rusty kettle.

The Way of Tea
and the Iemoto System

I n an autobiographical essay published in 1983, Hounsai wrote that becoming
iemoto was not an easy task. Becoming the Way of Tea meant undergoing a
physical and spiritual discipline with its own requisite traditions, philosophy,
and practice. It is Hounsai's sacred duty to preserve these traditions from a basis of
solid knowledge of the Way of Tea. Such responsibility requires a strong character
to speak and act with authority, organizing many people in Japan and abroad. It
means to transmit the Way of Tea to future generations of tea people and the next-
generation iemoto. It also meant adapting tea to the changing conditions of an
increasingly internationalized world while preserving its basic components.
Because of these heavy responsibilities, Hounsai has denied himself many of the
modern comforts and pleasures.

The iemoto system is as old as tea itself. It was created during Japan's feudal
period, from the thirteenth through the mid-nineteenth century, to protect the traditional arts from arbitrary, chaotic changes. The iemoto system arose out of the
need to preserve and stabilize the arts, functioning as a kind of ritual counterpart
to mechanisms to preserve political stability. Even before the term "iemoto" came
into use, the government established a system of controlling the ritual arts to prevent any deviation from political norms and avert any potential threat to the state.
The iemoto's *raison d'être* was to guarantee that the ritual expertise under his control was transmitted unchanged from generation to generation. Nevertheless, not
all iemoto-controlled arts survived; many of them, including their iemoto, fell victim to political vicissitudes. Tea was more fortunate, finding sponsors in each suc-
cessive period. To understand Hounsai's role as iemoto, we must first explore the
origins and the nature of the system itself.

In an effort to preserve the cultural orthodoxy and legitimacy of the ritual arts,
the iemoto strictly defined and controlled them through the system called *do* (way;

37

also pronounced *michi*). The Japanese have elevated many of their traditional arts and philosophy into "ways": *kado* is the Way of Poetry; *bushido*, the Way of the Samurai; *kendo*, the Way of the Sword; *shodo*, the Way of Calligraphy; *kado* (written differently from *kado*, the Way of Poetry), the Way of Flower Arranging; and *sado* (also *chado*), the Way of Tea. Consequently, "do" has become a distinct feature of traditional Japanese culture. Political sponsors tended to support the iemoto and the "way" he upheld as complementary and inseparable aspects of the art they sought to control. It was the notion of the way that allowed the iemoto to combine philosophy, ritual, and aesthetics into a single system.

Ever since the iemoto system was established, grand tea masters emphasized the practice of tea as a "way." Way means the practice of an art, not just as a skill, but as a philosophy, as a *way* of life. Chinese Taoists had already explained "do" as a way of life, as the art of being in this world . The term probably derives from a combination of the "way" (Ch., *dao*; Jp., *do*) and the somewhat later term, "Way of Buddhism," or *Butsudo*. When the grand tea masters claim their "way" as an avenue toward Buddhist enlightenment, they clearly follow in the footsteps of Taoist-Buddhist teaching and practice.

One of the main characteristics of this system of the "way" is that it required complete total commitment of its adherents. The grand tea masters enforce an "imitate the master" policy of learning. When asked how long such training takes, they invariably answer, "A lifetime." Cynical Westerners might speculate that this demand has at least some economic motivation, since lifelong students pay lifelong fees, but the insistence on complete, lifelong commitment actually derives from the model of Zen practice, in which one can only achieve ultimate emancipation through perfect self-discipline and complete immersion in and dedication to practice. Hounsai has said that only when one has mastered the art of tea can one be delivered from it. One must make it an integral part of one's being before one is allowed to express oneself through it. This way or "do" thereby becomes a kind of Butsudo, the discipline that Gautama Buddha engaged in before he attained the state of enlightenment.

It was Murata Juko who created the Way of Tea during the fifteenth century. Born in Nara, Juko entered the temple Shomyoji at an early age. When he was twenty-five he transferred to Kyoto, where he built himself a small hut in the bustling merchant quarter of the capital. He studied Zen at the temple Daitokuji under Priest Ikkyu Sojun and flower arranging under one of the *doboshu* (shogunal experts in the arts) before the celebrated poet and courtier Sanjonishi Sanetaka (1455–1537) introduced him to tea.

Juko created the Way of Tea on the basis of Butsudo, the Way of Buddhism. Tea for Juko was a means to gain enlightenment by upholding Buddhist ideals. His tea practice became religious practice. He wanted to restore spirituality and transcendental values to the practice of tea, which had deteriorated into a lavish entertainment of the shoguns and *daimyo*, or feudal lords. The *Wakan Chashi*, a history of Chinese and Japanese tea published in 1728, cites legends about Juko's tea as Buddhist practice:

> In the Bunmei era [1469–87] there lived a person named Juko. He lived at the temple Shomyoji in the Southern Capital [Nara]. He built a hut of miscanthus grass he had cut himself and called it a *sukiya*. He hung calligraphy on the wall and followed the path of the ancients and sought their truths. He looked for the plum blossoms already in the twelfth [lunar] month and tried to find chrysanthemums before it was autumn. He felt comfortable in this space as small as the inside of a bottle and lived there as if he were in a spacious hall. The mundane world left him unconcerned. He always kept his tea utensils ready for any guest at any time. [1]

He looked for flowers before their seasons, displaying buds to suggest the beauty of their future full bloom. The text later compares Juko's hut, "as narrow as the inside of a bottle," with that of Buddha's wealthy disciple Vimalakirti, who lived in a hut only ten feet square.

Juko was also one of the founders of the wabi aesthetic. Before the term wabi entered use, he borrowed the principles of "chilled and withered" from linked-verse (*renga*) poetry. In his *Kokoro no Fumi* (Heart's Note), addressed to the daimyo Furuichi Harima (1459–1508), Juko recommended the use of simple, Japanese-made utensils, but warned that their usage must be subject to the Zen spirit: "Again, at the same time, pretending, without anybody's recognition, to [have mastered the] 'chilled and withered,' [mere] beginners use such utensils as those made in Bizen and Shigaraki." For Juko, the use of wabi utensils was most difficult and not suitable for beginners. [2] Juko was referring to the linked-verse poet Sogi (1421–1502) who wrote, "When a person who is just beginning to study linked verse tries too hard to achieve a cold and withered style, . . . he will find it difficult to advance." [3] Juko wrote this at a time when tea masters still predominantly used Chinese tea utensils, following Chinese traditions of drinking tea. For Juko, using utensils of the "chill and withered" aesthetic was a way to "empty oneself" in the Buddhist spirit. Without that Buddhist spirit, the use of such utensils seemed absurd: "'Withered' means having good utensils, but 'chilled and lean' utensils only become interesting if one fully realizes their flavor, and this only after one has reached this state at the bottom of one's heart." [4]

Unfortunately, we know nothing about Juko's tea procedures, only about his tea philosophy as reported by later chroniclers. They unanimously describe Juko's tea as a world apart, a world evocative of enlightenment, eternity, peace, and art—values that are difficult to find in the ordinary, mundane world.

Under Takeno Jo'o, the Way of Tea matured. Jo'o was a third-generation disciple of Juko. He studied poetry, both *waka* (five lines of five, seven, five, seven, seven syllables) and linked-verse (waka composed in sequences) under Sanjonishi Sane-taka. He was born in 1502 and took the tonsure in 1532. He continued Juko's wabi tradition and wrote the *Jo'o Wabi no Fumi* (Jo'o's Letter on Wabi), leaving his disciples a set of twelve precepts stating that wabi was not just a fashionable aesthetic, but a way: "A tea that does not accord with the heart of the guest is not worthy of a man of tea (suki). Our tea solely seeks harmony with the heart of the guest and we consider it inappropriate to impose on the guest."[5] The host should only serve tea to a guest he knows intimately; otherwise it would not be a sincere tea. Tea as a way seems to go together with an identity called "man of tea" (suki), an expert in tea procedures and the selection and use of utensils, but also a spiritual leader, a transmitter of the way.

The practice of an art as a way and the iemoto system went hand in glove. The grand masters became promoters and the guardian-leaders of the way. Imbued with such authority, they defined not only what the way is, but also what the rules of its pursuit should be and how they should be kept.

The authority of the iemoto is an outgrowth of ritual. Since ritual participants perform a symbolic action, there needs to be a center of ritual authority. If ritual is freed from all restrictions, it will soon change so much that the connection between ritual and reality are lost. All ritual is subject to evolution and outside pressures, but there must be a central authority to ensure that the ritual does not lose its very purpose, and to adapt it appropriately to new circumstances. In most rituals, this function belongs to ritualists and priests; in tea it is the iemoto who exercises this authority. Before we examine the iemoto system specific to tea, it will be illuminating to observe how it developed in the world of Japanese court poetry.

State sponsorship of professionals or semi-professionals in the ritual arts is a precursor of the iemoto system. The heads of the Bureau of Poetry (Wakadokoro) and that of court music of the Heian-period (794–1185) imperial government saw to it that certain standards were upheld by entrusting artistic leadership to specific families. This was especially necessary for Chinese arts that had been transmitted to Japan and were maintained from generation to generation without the guidance of native Chinese teachers. For example, as early as the Nara period (710–84), the Toyohara family gained a monopoly over the teaching of the *sho*, originally a Chinese musical instrument used in the court music known as Gagaku.

Poetry was controlled through the practice of compiling imperial poetry anthologies. The poetry included in these anthologies was carefully selected for its suitability and its orthodox representation of seasonal changes and human sentiments. Inauspicious poetry was excluded as a threat to the state. The decline of the political power of the court in the twelfth and thirteenth centuries aroused the fear that court culture might also decline as a consequence, and the court subsequently developed high standards of poetry and poetry criticism to defend the art against such deterioration. The standards were set so high that only a handful of poets were deemed capable of upholding them.

The families of prominent poets allied themselves with powerful political factions, a policy that had the unfortunate consequence of involving them in the vicissitudes of politics. In order to secure the continuation of court poetry, therefore, Emperor Goreizei (1025–68) granted land to Fujiwara no Nagaie of the Mikohidari family so that the stable income from that land could sustain the family as professional poets. This family, however, declined his offer for political reasons, and by the end of the twelfth and beginning of the thirteenth century, the only remaining poet family was that of Fujiwara no Shunzei (1114–1204) and his son Teika and grandson Tameie (1198–1275). The descendants of this family shared unprecedented poetic authority, with the result that the authoritative medieval schools of court poetry such as the Nijo, Kyogoku, and Reizei schools all grew out of this single line. Supported by land holdings bestowed on them in perpetuity, these schools allied themselves with political groups and court factions and monopolized the compilation of imperial collections of poetry. After Teika compiled the *Shinkokinshu* (1205), the Nijo family became the major compilers, with the exception of the *Gyokuyoshu* and the *Fugashu* compiled by Kyogoku Tamekane (1254–1332).

The heads of these schools became the first iemoto in the field of poetry. There had been iemoto before but, as in the case of traditional families of imperial cooks or kickball athletes, they accepted disciples exclusively from courtiers and family members. The Nijo, Kyogoku, and Reizei schools differed in that they taught poetry to outsiders while at the same time maintaining a degree of control and leadership over the teacher-disciple relationship and poetic diction. The difference between this early system and the modern tea iemoto as it developed in the eighteenth century is that in the latter case disciples, once granted a license, could teach without the permission of the school and without paying portions of student fees to the school. The system of feudal lord-vassal relations that developed in twelfth-century Japan served as the model for teacher-disciple relations and became the backbone of the medieval iemoto system. Even after the leading Nijo family died out, the teacher-disciple system continued, but no longer under iemoto family control. This system, called *kokin denju*, consisted of imparting some of the secrets of Teika's poetry to the student. In possession of such secrets, the student was free to divulge the teachings as he saw fit. In this system of transmission, for example, there were fifty-four stages corresponding to the fifty-four chapters of the *Tale of Genji*, a novel written by Murasaki Shikibu at the beginning of the eleventh century. In order to be recognized as an accomplished master and teacher, one had to receive all fifty-four certificates, or *kirigami*, from a recognized master. Due to a very limited number of disciples in the feudal age, this system was sufficient to secure transmission of certain traditions at a satisfactory artistic level.

The ongoing development of the iemoto system carried over into the Ashikaga period. Jo'o received instruction in linked-verse poetry from Sanjonishi Sanetaka, paying him for a copy of a poetic text and for Sanetaka's corrections of the poems Jo'o had submitted for perusal. This indicates that a certain degree of artistic professionalization had taken shape under the influence of merchant patronage and the money economy that developed during the Ashikaga period. Professional or semi-professional poets such as Sanetaka and others were sponsored by the new merchant class as well as by warriors. Since Jo'o paid for Sanetaka's teachings, Jo'o's relationship with Sanetaka is a kind of early master-disciple relationship.[6]

Rikyu, too, received secret transmissions from his predecessors. Hideyoshi received the secret teachings about the use of the daisu table from Rikyu and, to enhance his authority in the Way of Tea, asked Rikyu not to divulge these teachings to anyone else. Hideyoshi then proceeded to transmit these teachings himself to his inner circle of loyal political allies and tea devotees including his nephew and appointed heir Toyotomi Hidetsugu (1568–95), Gamo Ujisato (1556–95), Hosokawa Sansai (1563–1645), Takayama Ukon (1553–1615), Seta Kamon (?–1595), and Shibayama Kenmotsu (dates uncertain). Hideyoshi permitted Rikyu to transmit the secret teachings only to Oda Uraku (1547–1621), Nobunaga's younger brother.[7] These examples demonstrate the extent of the political manipulation of the ritual arts. Hideyoshi, the supreme warlord, wanted to be seen not only as a military leader but as a ritual leader as well, as a way of legitimizing his temporal power.

Limiting the highest daisu teachings to a number of favorite disciples, Hideyoshi was in fact following an ancient practice called *hiden*, or "secret transmission." The secret transmission of documents and oral traditions was a major source of religious and artistic authority in premodern Japan. Authority was based on receiving secret teachings from a master, so in an attempt to ensure continuity, tea schools began to issue certificates to document that the bearer had received these teachings. Only the head of the school could bestow such a certificate on his chosen disciples. The certificate showed that the disciple had been granted the authority to teach and transmit the secret teachings to the next generation. The Reizei school of poetry drew its authority from the secret documents written by Teika in its possession. (These priceless documents were only recently made public.) In a culture where the arts had to be learned by the body, these certificates attested to a living embodiment of the art and not just an intellectual knowledge of it.

In seventeenth- and eighteenth-century tea these certificates did not prevent the disciples from transmitting the secret teachings they had received from their teachers to their own disciples and from creating their own schools. Rivalries between the schools proliferated. Twelve separate schools, patronized by different daimyo families, emerged from the Sekishu school alone.

The seventeenth century was quite different, however, from Rikyu's sixteenth century. In 1603, a new shogunal government (the third in Japanese history) was put in place. It came with a strict Confucian social stratification into four classes: warriors, peasants, artisans, and merchants. Warriors had to submit genealogies as proof that they deserved their social position. The shogunal government also regulated the relationship between daimyo and shogun through a system of reconfirmation reminiscent of the emerging iemoto system. Rikyu's disciples had to adapt their tea to the new social reality, hence the birth of the so-called "daimyo tea," a non-egalitarian, hierarchical tea that, unlike Rikyu's egalitarian wabi tea, reaffirmed the prevailing social structure in the tearoom. Wabi tea later staged a strong comeback under Sotan but, in the meantime, the control of tea shifted to Rikyu's first and second-generation daimyo disciples, such as Furuta Oribe, Kobori Enshu, and Enshu's disciple Katagiri Sekishu (1605–73). The Rikyu-Oribe-Enshu line of tea masters was based on Oribe's claim to have received Rikyu's secret teachings and Enshu's claim to have received these teachings through Oribe.

After Rikyu's death, Oribe taught tea to Toyotomi Hideyoshi and a number of Hideyoshi's daimyo. Hideyoshi encouraged Oribe to create a tea suited to the social order he sought to establish. This is perhaps why Oribe added a *shobanseki*, or "space for attendants," to his otherwise wabi-sized three-and-three-quarter-mat room. The shobanseki, separated from the main guests by sliding doors, is a space for the attendants of high-ranking participants. After Hideyoshi's death, Oribe went to Edo to teach the second shogun, but he was forced into suicide in 1615 by the retired first shogun, Tokugawa Ieyasu (1542–1616). Kobori Enshu was then asked to become the official teacher to the third shogun, and his disciple Sekishu taught the fourth shogun. From the fourth shogun until the end of the Tokugawa period in 1868, Sekishu's tea, which was compatible with the new social system, became the shogunal tradition. Other daimyo also switched to the Sekishu school, which, with its highly formal tea and shogunal patronage, exhibited a strong sectarian consciousness that did not exist in Rikyu's time. The *Sanbyaku Kajo* (Three Hundred Rules) of the Sekishu school became the school's primary text.

The Sen school (Senke) staged a comeback under Sen Sotan, Rikyu's grandson. With the increasing prestige that Rikyu came to enjoy as the years after his death passed and the strong system of family lineage enforced by the Tokugawa shoguns, Sotan came to be recognized as Rikyu's legitimate blood relative and successor. Despite Sotan's emphasis on wabi, the Senke schools, too, had to adapt to the new social reality. While integrating the formalities of the social hierarchy into tea, they continued to stress egalitarianism. Sotan continued Rikyu's egalitarian tea but he did all in his power to place his sons in prominent positions with other feudal lords, despite the fact that they would have to engage in the non-egalitarian daimyo tea. His second son, Soshu, the founder of the Mushanokoji Senke school, took employment with the daimyo Matsudaira of Takamatsu on Shikoku island; his third son, Sosa, the founder of the Omote Senke school, served the Tokugawa branch family centered in Kii Province; and his fourth son, Soshitsu, the founder of the Urasenke school, went to teach tea to the powerful Maeda family of Kaga Province. Two of Sotan's favorite disciples also found employment with prominent daimyo: Yamada Sohen with the Yoshida family of Mikawa Province and Fujimura Yoken with the Todo family of Iga Province. In their competition for employment, there was considerable infighting among family members and disciples over who was the most legitimate successor of a school. Such infighting contributed to the establishment of separate schools, supported by claims of secret teachings and the publication of genealogies and pamphlets.

Unlike other tea schools, the Senke schools, despite their procedural differences, remained committed to each other's welfare; they were bound together by the weight of Rikyu's authority. One area in which this became particularly apparent was the custom of adopting each other's children whenever a school faced the danger of dying out. Over ten such adoptive transactions are recorded over the course of Senke history. Sotan also issued certificates to a number of disciples who founded their own schools and descent lines, often in the provinces. In Sotan's time this kind of direct teacher-disciple relationship usually lasted only one generation; loyalty to the school that had issued one's certificate did not develop until the iemoto system was fully in place. Whereas other schools had already begun issuing certificates upon receiving pledges of loyalty, such absolute school loyalty was no doubt contrary to Sotan's wabi spirit. His tea was a kind of "no-school" tea. The three Senke schools did not became firmly established as separate schools of tea until as late as 1740, nearly a century after the death of Sotan. Perhaps the schools finally separated only because of outside pressures and patronage.

Sotan's fourth son, Soshitsu, did not stay long in Maeda's service, preferring to remain in Kyoto and continue his father's wabi tea. This independence was made possible by the increasing number of Kyoto merchants seeking instruction in wabi tea. At the bottom of the Tokugawa social scale, merchants were either unable or reluctant to engage in the lavish daimyo tea and preferred the frugal wabi tea as appropriate to their low social station. Goods were confiscated from a number of merchants who had grown too rich in the eyes of the shogunal government or who had made a public display of their wealth, so merchants were attracted to the frugal wabi tea as a safer and more congenial practice.

Merchants also welcomed the egalitarianism of wabi tea, which offered them a way to escape from the rigid social structure of their day. They practiced tea as an expression of resistance to and liberation from their low social status. This return to wabi also explains the popularity of the Yabunouchi school, which drew its main support from the merchants, but also from the adepts of the True Pure Land (Jodo Shin Shu) sect of Buddhism. This return to wabi did not go without criticism;

Konoe Iehiro (1667–1736), a courtier, criticized Senke ignorance of social status and the filthy wabi custom of deliberately spilling water over the tatami mat when pouring water into the tea bowl. [8]

The monopolistic iemoto system as we know it today developed as a means to prevent the endless proliferation of schools and to subject the ever-increasing number of tea practitioners to feudal control, especially the merchants and people in the provinces. Schools therefore began to limit the number of certificates they issued. Former disciples were no longer allowed to issue their own certificates and all certificates had to be sanctioned or issued by the iemoto or their legitimate heirs. Only the iemoto received what was called "complete transmission" (*kanzen soden*) together with the school-specific secret teachings. This invested the iemoto with absolute and unquestionable authority. A disciple received only an "incomplete transmission (*fukanzen soden*) as a license to teach on behalf of the iemoto. This incomplete transmission did not include the secret teachings restricted to the iemoto. Provided with such authority, the iemoto were able to control their disciples as well as the tea procedures and use of utensils.

The structure of the iemoto system parallels the structural relations found in Buddhist institutions between main (*honzan*) and branch (*matsuji*) temples and in the family system between main (*honke*) and branch (*bunke*) families. When religious and social institutions split into branches it is necessary to create legitimate links between the main body and its branches. Temple and shrine support groups (such as Ise Oshi, Kumano Goshi, Honganji Monto) were also organized in a system resembling that of the iemoto. This structure spilled over into the Noh and Kyogen theaters, tea, and other arts.

The iemoto system was adopted by the martial arts such as archery, swordsmanship, horsemanship, lance fighting, and sharpshooting, and even schools of philosophy and thought, such as Confucianism, yin-yang divination, and the military and navigational sciences. When the merchants started learning poetry such as linked verse and comic verse (*haikai*), and patronizing theatrical arts such as Kabuki and Bunraku, they introduced an iemoto system into them, often based on transmissions of secret teachings. The woodblock print artist Hokusai was looked upon as an iemoto by his students, and gardeners, architects, and the makers of tea utensils were organized into iemoto-type groups such as the Senke Jusshoku, or "Ten Artisans of the Sen Family."

The first person to establish this kind of iemoto system in tea was the fifth Yabunouchi school head Fujusai Chikushin (1678–1745), who was probably inspired by the system of authority that Nishi Honganji's high priest exercised over his believers. The high priest passed on special teachings to his favorite disciples, who could then claim spiritual authority on the basis of having received these teachings. Fujusai Chikushin gave a portion of his name to his disciples and had them pledge loyalty to the school, preventing them from establishing their own schools and their own procedures. The disciples had to pay fees that ensured a stabilized income for the school head. In addition to the certificates of the secret transmission they had received, the school heads also drew authority from membership in their own blood or artistic genealogies, as well as from ritual acts of worship of the school's ancestor.

Certain tea procedures can be performed only by the iemoto. For example, the offertory teas (*kucha* or *kencha*) regularly presented to temples and shrines must be performed by the grand master; no one else is allowed to practice this ritual, even though observers could easily memorize and imitate it. Part of the iemoto's authority is derived precisely from the fact that certain tea procedures are an exclusive family monopoly, recognized not only by other tea practitioners but by political leaders and the public as well. Iemoto also exercised their authority by affixing their signature of authentication to boxes containing tea utensils, a practice called *hakogaki*, or "box signing." A tea utensil bearing an iemoto's signature is worth much more than an unsigned one, and iemoto often presented all attendants with a utensil of their design and signature after memorial services to their ancestors.

The first such iemoto in the Senke lineage was Omote Senke's seventh head, Joshinsai (d. 1751) and his younger brother, Urasenke's fifth head, Yugensai (d. 1771). Nevertheless, Joshinsai made one exception. He dispatched his favorite disciple Kawakami Fuhaku (1716–1807) to Edo, where Fuhaku founded the still thriving Edo Senke school. Okakura Tenshin, the celebrated author of *The Book of Tea*, is a descendant of Kawakami Fuhaku.

The new iemoto system had other important attributes, such as the introduction of the drill-like Seven Ceremonies (*Shichijishiki*). These ceremonies begin with the still-popular kagetsu, in which five people draw lots and take turns in preparing and drinking tea. The ceremony was instituted to make tea instruction more pleasant and appealing to the merchants, but was criticized by other schools for its disregard of differences in social status. It was not until the daimyo and tea man Ii Naosuke that tea egalitarianism was recognized by a leading daimyo as a virtue.

As mentioned above, to be credible, the iemoto system required that the house or lineage be founded by a person of unusual virtue. Thus the Reizei school of poetry draws its claim to authority from the accomplished poetry of Fujiwara no Shunzei and, in particular, Teika. The Ikenobo school of flower arrangement claims as its ancestor Ikenobo Senkei (fifteenth century), whose skills in arranging flowers each morning at the Kyoto temple Rokkakudo has become a tradition emulated by followers until the present. The Senke schools of tea claim Rikyu as their founder; but why not Rikyu's predecessors Murata Juko or Takeno Jo'o, or even his alleged direct ancestor, the doboshu Sen'ami? One answer to this question is that Rikyu's special skills and revolutionary changes in tea entitled him to the status of founder of the Senke schools of tea, but it is also true that his tragic death—

Toyotomi Hideyoshi forced him to commit suicide—added to his appeal. Tragic heroes such as Sugawara Michizane (845–903) and Minamoto Yoshitsune (1159–89), and later Saigo Takamori (1827–77) and Nogi Maresuke (1849–1912) were deified and became the objects of widespread popular worship. Sugawara Michizane became Tenjin, the god of literature, and Rikyu became the god of tea. The *Nanboroku* suggests that by the hundredth anniversary of Rikyu's death Rikyu had already assumed the role of tutelary deity of tea.[9] Now all Senke iemoto, including of course Hounsai, offer Rikyu regular worship and honor him at the anniversary of his death with tea and visits to his grave. The worship of Rikyu is the backbone of the Senke iemoto system.

By the end of the seventeenth century, when the iemoto system was established, tea had come to be considered part of the public, not the private realm. As such, tea had to comply with public norms, and deviation was condemned as heresy and severely punished. Government officials regarded any heterodox behavior as a potential threat to public order and political authority. Hence, the political sponsorship of the iemoto system developed as a part of a broader strategy to control society by uniting people through government-sponsored arts. Matsudaira Fumai (1751–1818), a great collector of tea utensils and Sekishu school adherent, expressed this clearly in his *Mudagoto* (Superfluous Things) written at the age of nineteen, three years before he became a successful daimyo:

> In our generation, everyone tries to engage in tea solely for the purpose of amusement, whereas, in fact, it should be practiced to help one in governing the nation. It should be pursued to achieve harmony by purifying one's heart and by establishing courtesy and unity among all people, high and low. If one lets tea help in governing the country, then, without doubt, one gets good people. . . . Even when one is preoccupied with small matters, it can help one to govern the country. Even Ieyasu liked tea and used it as a means to unite the nation and to create harmony. . . . This is what a great leader should do.[10]

Like his contemporary, the chief shogunal advisor Matsudaira Sadanobu (1758–1829), Fumai stressed the potential of tea to preserve the social order. Wabi tea, which provided a good example of public frugality and simplicity, staged a comeback due to Sadanobu's strict sumptuary laws against luxury and waste.

As the iemoto system flourished, many books on tea appeared and proper knowledge of tea procedures became a requirement for the well educated in Tokugawa-period society. The *Sojinboku* of 1626 is a forerunner of a tea-related publication boom that occurred during the Genroku period (1688–1704). Yamada Sohen (1627–1708), one of Sotan's Four Favorite Disciples and tea master to the Ogasawara daimyo family, published three books on tea.[11] Endo Genkan (dates unknown) published six books. [12] All are testimonies to the increasing concern over correct tea procedures. Even such famous authors as Kaibara Ekiken (1630–1714) wrote on tea. His *Sarei Kuketsu* of 1699 addressed itself to a samurai readership. In the preface, Ekiken warns his readers that: "even the brave samurai who do not know how to behave in a reception are shameful and unsightly." [13]

But arts closely linked with political power also decline with that power. The various tea schools keenly felt the loss of daimyo and shogunal sponsorship after the demise of the Tokugawa regime in the late 1860s and during the subsequent Meiji period (1868–1912). The Urasenke school survived mainly thanks to grand master Gengensai's foresight and innovations and Yumyosai's efforts to include tea in the curriculum of girls' schools. Since the Tokugawa excluded women from public functions, they were not allowed to practice tea openly. Sugiki Fusai (1628–1706), one of the famous disciples of Sotan, completely excluded women from tea. An exception was in the pleasure quarters, where the social order was often reversed, and courtesans served tea to their male customers.

The merchant houses also continued to sponsor tea in the Meiji period. Masuda Don'o (1847–1938) of Mitsui and Iwasaki Yanosuke (1851–1908), younger brother of Yataro, the founder of Mitsubishi, were avid collectors of tea utensils. Don'o held tea gatherings annually at his private residence in Tokyo and is recorded to have held more than one thousand tea parties, equaled only by the Tokugawa-period daimyo Kobori Enshu and Matsudaira Fumai.

The iemoto system evolved to become the type of system that Hounsai embodies over a long and complex history spanning many generations. Looking back on this history, Hounsai pointed out some of the landmarks in the more recent development of the iemoto system: (1) the conservative feudal system of the Tokugawa period; (2) the will of the Meiji government to save traditional culture from the onslaught of Western civilization; (3) the efforts many modern Japanese make to find their cultural identity in the traditional arts such as tea; and (4) his personal efforts to keep tea within the realm of religion and to live tea as part of himself.

Teahuts and Tea Rooms

There are two types of tea rooms, the shoin reception room and the small wabi room. As we have already learned, the wabi room developed as a smaller, less formal version of the shoin room. Hounsai maintains that the four-and-a-half-mat room is a compromise between the two styles. Although there are four-and-a-half-mat rooms in both the shoin and wabi styles, the shoin room is usually larger and the wabi room smaller. The small room is a miniature version of the large one and is based on a different philosophy. From Rikyu's time to Hounsai's modern practice of tea, most tea people used both shoin- and wabi-style rooms to serve tea, depending on the number and the status of their guests. As we learned earlier, shoin tea was a ritual that reaffirmed social hierarchy, while wabi tea came to symbolize social equality and individual spirituality. The relative paucity of treatises on the shoin room suggests that the smaller wabi room presented a greater ethical and aesthetic challenge than the larger room. These two room types also came to represent two varying styles of tea, usually called shoin tea and wabi tea. Both types of tea room owe their basic shapes and dimensions to architectural developments of the Kamakura and following Ashikaga periods. Let us begin with the development of the shoin tea room.

The earliest type of tea meeting still practiced is the commemoration of the death of the monk Eisai, which is held every year on April 20 at the Kenninji temple in Kyoto. The hall in which this tea is held reveals the characteristic architectural environment for serving tea in the Kamakura period. Both the architectural features and the procedures of the memorial tea are strongly influenced by Chinese styles. In the middle of the temple hall, monks place four seats for the four main guests. They face each other from east and west with the altar placed at the hall's northern wall. A portrait of Eisai hangs in the middle. Monks serve tea in Chinese-style bowls on trays, first to the altar and then to the guests.

While tea was served in such temple halls, some early tea devotees also availed themselves of the aristocratic *shinden*-style of architecture exemplified in the palaces and mansions of Heian-period Kyoto. Sasaki Doyo (1296–1373), an extravagant warrior known for his lavish parties, imitated the Chinese style of serving tea, but not the Buddhist architecture of, for example, Eisai's Kenninji.[1] To compete with the governor,[2] Doyo said he would decorate seven rooms, prepare seven types of food, offer seven hundred sorts of prizes, and hold seventy rounds of tea contests.[3] What kind of rooms Doyo decorated we do not know, but the seven rooms may have been an imitation of the aristocratic shinden, which had wings attached to both sides of a central main hall.

We learn a little more about tea architecture during the Ashikaga period from a text entitled *Muromachidono Gyoko Okazari Ki*, which describes the decorations used during the visit of Emperor Gohanazono to the shogunal residence Muromachidono on October 21 to 26, 1437.[4] The architecture of the Muromachidono, built around a pond, recalls the water pavilions of Chinese mansions and palaces, pavilions that were used only for artistic pursuits and for entertaining guests. In the Chinese tradition, the entertainment of guests and the pursuit of the arts required a separate architecture and special landscaping.

The emperor visited a number of reception halls called *kaisho*, which had been similarly decorated with paintings of Buddhas, bodhisattvas, and tigers and dragons, but included separate tea parlors lacking in Kenninji. These tea parlors were used for the display of precious Chinese tea utensils and for serving tea. As at Kenninji, the guests—here the emperor and his followers—sat on chairs imported from China. Some of the rooms had built-in writing desks and split-level shelves and *oshi ita*, a low decorative platform that later developed into the tokonoma alcove. The floors were wooden, covered at best with some kind of simple straw matting, as tatami mats were not yet in use. At Sasaki Doyo's party the floors were covered with animal skins.

An important element of the history of tea architecture is the fact that reception buildings contained tea rooms, that is, special rooms built and arranged for the serving of tea. Tea and the collection of tea utensils required a separate architectural style. Let us take one room called the Shinzo Kaisho (Newly Built Meeting Place) as an example of Ashikaga-period interior architecture and decoration.

In the Small Bird Alcove hung the scroll painting *Shakyamuni Leaving the Mountain* by Liang Kai, flanked by a pair of scroll paintings of snowy landscapes. In front of this triptych stood a carved table finished in red lacquer on which was displayed the standard set of three implements (incense container, heron, and turtle). On each side of these were two bronze vases. The split-level shelves featured a cup with a design of human figures, a food box with a painting of Fukurokuju, the Chinese god of wealth and longevity, and other objects placed on carved red lacquer trays with designs of hawks and cranes. Hawks are symbols of warrior audacity and strength and cranes are symbols of longevity. On the built-in desk (*tsukeshoin*), there was a carved red lacquer box containing an inkstone, a brush rack with a dragon pattern, and a painting of cranes by Wei Tsong (Jp., Kiso, a Chinese emperor of the Northern Song dynasty and painter, 1082–1135). In this room alone, some forty Chinese art objects were on display, including four paintings. Priest Mansai who saw the display wrote his impressions in his diary: " When I saw the rooms, I could not believe my eyes. There was no end to the splendor and beauty and it is hard to describe it in words."[5]

Perhaps in presenting such a luxurious artistic display the shogun wished to convey the message that the shoguns offered paradise on earth. For example, records show that the Kinkaku (Golden Pavilion), built in 1397 by the third Ashikaga shogun Yoshimitsu, was designed to be an earthly copy of Amida's Western Paradise.

The arrangement of the rooms of the Muromachidono suggests that the buildings were divided into formal, public rooms and more private ones. The northern tea rooms, which seem less formal than the southern ones, were probably used for tea contests (*tocha*). Popular among the warriors, tea contests consisted in drinking a cup of tea and then two more, commenting on the quality and provenance of the latter two in comparison with the first.[6] Some of these rooms were small, four-mat rooms, as in the Minamimuki Kaisho, the south-facing reception building. In contrast, the North Tea Chamber came with a lower-floor adjacent room to the north of the main room. It is conceivable that this lower-floor room functioned as a place where guests could wash their hands and stretch their legs, as in the roji used in later centuries.

Perhaps these northern tea rooms are the precursors of what is known as "the tea room in the back," where the Sakai merchants served tea after meals during the sixteenth century. It is also interesting to note that the more specialized tea rooms faced north. Because they tend to let in less daylight, tea rooms facing north were more suited for the appreciation of tea utensils and other works of art. Perhaps this design was also a means to protect the decorative utensils from too much light. In later tea history, the notion that tea utensils were considered more beautiful in shadows than in clear daylight becomes more explicit. For example, the *Ikenaga Sosa e no Sho*, a letter written by Takeno Jo'o for his disciple Ikenaga Sosa, says: "A tea room should be built toward the north. The reasons for this are to prevent strong light from entering, and to let in just enough to see the utensils. The light from the east, west, south, and north varies. When there is too much light, the utensils become too clearly visible."[7] From the Ashikaga Period onward, the control of light in tea rooms became a concern of tea architecture.[8]

Tea would never have developed as it did without tatami mats. It would have continued to be served on chairs or to guests seated on the wooden floors, as it was in China and in Zen temples. In the Higashiyama period (1436–90), the introduction of the shoin style of architecture had a decisive influence on the development of tea as we know it today. The room called Dojinsai of a hall named Togudo of the Silver Pavilion in Kyoto is the earliest extant shoin-style room in Japan. The Togudo was built in 1485 at the behest of the eighth shogun, Ashikaga Yoshimasa (1436–90), as a private chapel with a Buddhist altar room. The floor is covered by four and one-half tatami mats, and there is a board or low desk in front of paper windows used for reading and writing (hence the name shoin, meaning "study"). Although the room has split-level shelves, there is no tokonoma recess. Perhaps decorative scrolls were hung on one of the cross beams between the pillars, as was common in temple halls. The room was no doubt used also as a library, as evidenced by its split-level shelves and reading facility. Sliding doors provide a greater degree of privacy and intimacy than in aristocratic shinden halls, where separate rooms are created by hanging curtains or placing standing screens.[9] Shoin architecture was the first to divide the interior into separate rooms by the use of sliding doors. These sliding doors, however, were not complete room dividers because they did not extend all the way to the ceiling, but left a portion open above, occupied by a railing often decorated with carvings or lattice. The shoin provided more privacy than the shinden style, although one could still hear what was being said in the adjacent rooms or hallways through the open railing at the top. The two styles are similar in their flexibility, since the sliding doors of shoin architecture could be removed to create one big, open hall stretching out unhindered between the roof-supporting pillars, as in the shinden style.

Scholars believed that the Dojinsai had been used as a room for Buddhist practice and meditation, but archeologists have recently discovered an ancient hearth that indicates that this room may have been used for the preparation of tea, either to offer to the Buddha or for personal enjoyment. João Rodrigues, however, disagrees:

> He [Ashikaga Yoshimasa] built there a small house which was used exclusively for gatherings to drink tea. He assembled all the utensils needed for such meetings: a copper stove, a cast-iron kettle, a tea caddy, a cane brush, a small spoon, and porcelain cups from which to drink the tea. The house was only four and one-half mats in size and was constructed of drab materials. To compensate for this plainness, he chose the utensils carefully, insisting on special proportions, sizes, and shapes, and hung monochrome ink paintings in the alcove.[10]

Shoin tea during the Higashiyama period made use of a decorative space called the tokonoma. This was used for the display of a variety of art objects, including Chinese paintings or calligraphy, a flower arrangement, an incense container, and a candle holder (often in the form of a turtle and a crane, two Chinese symbols of longevity). Calligraphy, however, became the centerpiece of tokonoma decoration. Calligraphy, usually produced by Zen monks, gave tea a philosophical and religious depth and kept it from becoming a mere ceremony. The host's symbolic expression of his thoughts through his choice of tokonoma decorations became an indispensable feature of tea.

Tokonoma decorations had first developed out of the display of scrolls of calligraphy, paintings, and Buddhist implements in Zen temples. The first type of tokonoma consisted of tables placed against the walls bearing flowers, candlesticks, censers, and similar objects. These were placed in front of Buddhist scrolls in square or rectangular temple halls. In time, these altar tables became architecturally integrated into the room and built at a higher level than the rest of the room. According to the *Kissa Orai*, a book about the origins of tea written in the first half of the sixteenth century, the paintings displayed in a tea pavilion were all on Buddhist subjects: Shakyamuni and Avalokiteshvara hung on the front wall, flanked by paintings of Manjushri and Samantabhadra. Under the influence of tea, however, the place where these implements were displayed assumed an aura of sacredness comparable to that of an altar, commanding the same degree of reverence as if religious objects were displayed there. No one would dare to step, let alone sit, on the tokonoma. In tea, however, objects of aesthetic appreciation replaced the religious implements. The tokonoma was essential for tea men who possessed important collections of Chinese and Japanese utensils and wished to express their highly personal aesthetic taste, wealth, and social status by displaying them. The tokonoma became an indispensable element of ritualized social relations centered upon the aesthetic appreciation of utensils. Exactly the same motivation was at work in European royal palaces and the residences of the nobles; what was displayed in the galleries and cupboards was considered art precisely because it was displayed as such.

Especially in shoin settings, the Chinese utensils and paintings on display expressed the power and social status of the tea master. Shoin tea reinforced social distinctions, a departure from the religious message of the equality of all before the Buddhas that was expressed in the Buddhist setting at the Dojinsai. The shoin maintained this ritual function for many centuries to come, remaining distinct from tea of the "small room," with its emphasis on equality.

According to Hounsai, small rooms developed from two possible sources. One source is the cubicle created in the shoin by placing standing screens, as in Heian-period palace architecture. An eighteen-mat shoin room could thus be subdivided into four quasi-separate rooms with an area of roughly four and one-half mats each. The four mats, Hounsai maintains, represent the four seasons and the half-mat the the in-between seasons called doyo.

Hounsai claims that the *hojo*, the abbot's four-and-one-half-mat room in Zen temples, may be another model for the small tea room. The hojo is believed to have been named after Vimalakirti's ten-foot by ten-foot room, to which he invited eighty-four thousand bodhisattvas in the *Vimalakirti-nirdesa-sutra*. For Vimalakirti, the small room contained infinite space and was a world unto itself, where the continuity of ordinary space and time, dependent on our physical existence, ceases to exist. Within such a room, one is unencumbered by material limitations. There is no absolute time, only the ever-changing now. For a person trained in Zen, a small, cramped four-and-one-half-mat room can be transformed into infinite space and freedom.

At a deeper level, the small tea room can be traced back to the Buddhist notion of a religious retreat. The retreat is the ideal place—a forest, a tranquil place, a place beyond but not too far away from human habitation. There one undertakes twelve special practices to rid oneself of the Twelve Attachments to clothing, food, and shelter that hinder enlightenment (Jp., *juni zuda*; Skt., *dhavasa dhutagunah*). Two of these twelve practices are "taking any seat one may be offered" and "using the same seat for both eating and meditation."[11]

Ultimately, the small room coincides with the advent and popularity of wabi tea. Hence the custom arose of using only natural elements such as bamboo, reed, and clay in building wabi tea rooms. The tokonoma posts were installed with the bark still on to give the tea room a rustic look.

According to extant documents, Sanjonishi Sanetaka was the first person to build a four-and-one-half-mat tea room in the shoin style on his estate. In June 1502, he purchased a hut of six mats in Kyoto, moved it to his estate on Mushanokoji street, and rebuilt it in the reduced size of four and one-half mats. He gave it the name Sumiya (Corner Hut), landscaped it with rocks and trees, and surrounded it with a fence to suggest a mountain hut apart from the bustling world. He built it in the style of the hut of a hermit who has retired from the mundane world. One of Sanetaka's acquaintances, Toyohara Sumiaki, built a rustic hut under a pine tree in the rear of his garden and called it Yamazatoan (Mountain Village Hut), probably because it looked like a mountain retreat. This, too, was probably a tea room in the shoin style. He was followed by Murata Soshu, Murata Juko's disciple, who built a similar hut, called Goshoan (High-Noon Pine Tree Hut) in the lively merchant quarters of lower Kyoto (Shimogyo). In his diary, the poet Socho described the hut as a four-and-one-half-mat room: "In Shimogyo nowadays, there is a tea they call suki that takes place in either a four-and-one-half-mat or a six-mat room. I entered Soshu's gate and there was a big pine and a cedar tree. Inside the fence everything was clean."

The trees must have made Socho feel as if he were deep in the countryside, whereas he was in the middle of the bustling city. Socho was particularly impressed with five or six colored ivy leaves that had fallen on the ground, and he composed the following poem:

> *This morning,*
> *I picked up last night's storm—*
> *The first red leaves.*[12]

Jo'o, the teacher of Rikyu, also built himself a mountain retreat, called Daikokuan (Hut of the God of Wealth) inside the city. He had studied poetry under Sanjonishi Sanetaka and settled in the commercial quarters of Kyoto, not far from Soshu's abode. Jo'o returned to Sakai when the Hokke Uprising erupted in Kyoto in 1536 and all the Nichiren temples, which were supported by the merchants, were burned down by the monks of Enryakuji temple on Mount Hiei. When the Onin Wars broke out ten years later, Kyoto turned into a battleground, and many tea devotees fled to the safety of the city of Sakai. Dubbed the Venice of Japan by Catholic missionaries, Sakai offered more security than the politically divided capital because of its relative autonomy and the fact that it was administered as a republic.

In Sakai, wealthy merchants like Tsuda Sotatsu (1504–66) of the Tennojiya shop, his son, Sogyu (d. 1591), and Jo'o's son-in-law Imai Sokyu (1520–93) adopted Jo'o's wabi tea and built "mountain retreats" in the city. João Rodrigues, in a section of his *History of the Church in Japan* (*História de Igreja do Japão*) entitled "About the New Popular Style of Tea Called Suki and Its Origins and Ideals in General," observed: "Because of the lack of space within the city [of Sakai], they made certain changes such as reducing the size of the teahouse, and entertained their friends in these cha houses within the city itself."[13] For Rodrigues, a first-hand observer, it appeared that the Sakai tea people built small teahouses out of sheer necessity. In his descriptions of the way these tea huts were built, however, we find not only necessity but also a philosophy.

> Emphasis is laid on a frugal and an apparently natural setting; nothing fashionable or elegant is used, but only utensils in keeping with a hermit's retreat. Social distinctions are not observed in this wholesome pastime, and a lower-ranking person may invite a lord or a noble, who on such occasion will behave as an equal. . . . The thatched cha house is small, from one-and-a-half to four mats in size, and is constructed of old wood; the ceiling is made of coarse woven reeds, smoke-dried to show age and lonely poverty.[14]

Under Toyotomi Hideyoshi's reign, the shoin and the wabi styles merged to create a new, mixed style. For example, when Hideyoshi had just been awarded the title of Kanpaku (regent), the highest rank in the emperor's government, he served tea to the emperor in a three-mat tea room made of gold. The size of the room suggests an intimacy rather inappropriate for a subject serving tea to an emperor, but the tea hut was covered with gold leaf. The message of the tea setting was clear: it symbolized Hideyoshi's power and wealth and, by associating himself in this manner with the emperor, it helped legitimize Hideyoshi's political authority and project this message to the populace of Japan. When this golden tea hut was later displayed at Hideyoshi's Osaka castle, the warriors who inspected it were impressed by Hideyoshi's imperial association and wealth. The golden hut achieved Hideyoshi's goal of political hegemony by providing a suitable ritual site. He later used the golden hut to display his collection of precious tea utensils to the public. Out of respect to the emperor, however, this tea hut was never again used to serve tea to guests.

Perhaps under the influence of Sen Rikyu, Hideyoshi developed a predilection for small tea rooms. His famous Yamazato at Osaka Castle, built in 1583, was a four-and-one-half-mat room. Like the hermitage in the city, this was a hermitage within castle walls. Rikyu's Taian (Waiting [for Hideyoshi] Hut) was even smaller: a two-and-one-half-mat hut. It had a small nijiriguchi entrance only 78.8 centimeters high and 71.5 centimeters wide. It also had a *shitajimado* window, an opening in the wall, covered on the inside with reed and bamboo and on the outside with paper. This only provided light and could not be opened to produce a view. This construction clearly and radically demarcated the outside and the inside, the mundane world and a religious world of essential equality and spirituality. Hideyoshi loved to serve tea in small rooms, especially when he wanted to create intimacy and familiarity with his allies. Hideyoshi invited his guests occasionally to one of his large shoin tea rooms, only to invite them once more to the intimacy of his small Yamazato at Osaka Castle.

When Rikyu was nearing seventy (an exceptional longevity considering the average age at that time in Japan), he built himself a one-and-one-half-mat room at Hideyoshi's Jurakutei Castle in Kyoto. According to Rikyu's disciple Yamanoue Soji, this was an eccentric tea room built by an eccentric tea master: "Soeki [Rikyu] built the first ever one-and-one-half-mat room in Kyoto. This was unusual at the time and not meant for ordinary people. Rikyu, however, was an expert and, as if he were placing a mountain into the valley, or west into east, he broke the rules of tea and practiced it freely but interestingly. If ordinary persons were to do as Soeki did, there would no longer be tea as we know it."[15]

According to Yamanoue Soji, there were prior attempts to build small rooms. For example, he mentions the three-mat suki room that had allegedly existed before Jo'o, who reduced it to a two-mat room. Such small rooms suggest retirement from the mundane world, secluding oneself in an environment so small that it can fit only one person; the host is his own guest. People meet there as spirits sharing in the celebration of the moment. Rikyu considered this the ultimate expression of wabi philosophy. Rikyu's grandson Sotan was to build another one-and-one-half-mat room called Konnichian (Today's Hut), as a sign of ultimate retirement and seclusion.

As the Tokugawa shoguns set up a new social order, it became increasingly difficult and even dangerous to create heterodox art or engage in idiosyncratic behavior. The eccentric and free behavior that was tolerated during periods of political disorganization was now coming to an end. The Tokugawa regime encouraged artists to comply with accepted, legitimate norms. Rikyu's disciples served tea more often in the shoin environment to confirm the new social order. Kobori Enshu, a daimyo of many talents, sometimes served tea in a small room, but on these occasions he used an Oribe-style shoin room called *kusarinoma* for after-tea meetings. Enshu, who designed the garden of the Nijo Castle as well as the shogun's castle in Kyoto and the Shokintei teahouse of Katsura Imperial Villa, built a teahouse at Ryokoin, a subtemple of the Daitokuji. This teahouse, named Mittan, was a model of his taste and established the design of teahouses to come. He built it in the four-and-three-quarter-mat shoin style with split-level shelves, a reading platform, and a tokonoma. The three-quarter-size mat is used by the host to prepare tea. The Bosenseki tea room in the Kohoan subtemple of the Daitokuji, built late in his life, contained a twelve-mat shoin-style room. Of course, many features are reminiscent of Rikyu's wabi-style huts with their small nijiriguchi and beautifully arranged roji paths and gardens. Enshu's tea rooms comply with the requirements of Tokugawa social order while retaining elements of Rikyu's wabi aesthetic.

Rikyu's wabi style, however, did not die out completely. It was revived in the Tokugawa period by his grandson Sotan and, in the Meiji period, by Matsuura Takeshiro (1818–88), the Hokkaido explorer. Matsuura built a one-mat room called Taizanso (presently at International Christian University, Tokyo). Here he was able to prepare tea only for himself. What a contrast a one-mat room must have been for an explorer of a territory as vast as Hokkaido! These tea rooms are illustrations of the Japanese fascination for the miniature.

Teahouses and rooms in the Urasenke compound reflect the major styles of tea architecture through the ages. The Kan'untei is an eight-mat shoin-style room built according to the tastes of Sotan. It is located in the same building as the Konnichian. The Yuin is a four-and-one-half-mat house Sotan built for his retirement in imitation of Rikyu's four-and-one-half-mat room at Jurakutei Castle. With its thatched roof, it gives one the impression of a hermitage in a bustling city. Hounsai describes it as a unique and compact room that "makes me feel at ease. . . . It is neither too large nor too small."[16] The Totsutotsusai consists of two rooms, one of eight mats and the other of six, which can be connected by removing the sliding doors separating them. Perhaps because of its size and adaptability, this room has become the main teaching room at Urasenke. It is also the room where Hounsai serves tea to his most important guests: royalty, heads of state, and high-ranking government officials. The alcove post is made of the trunk of a pine tree that the eighth-generation Yugensai had once planted at Daitokuji. The fourteen-mat Tairyuken room was built by Ennosai to commemorate his fifty-second birthday and the birth of his grandson, Hounsai. This, too, is a shoin-style room. It is a formal reception room, the largest in the Urasenke complex, but it is built only from materials that are usually used for wabi teahuts. When one removes the sliding doors on all three sides, the size of the room almost doubles. With the writing desk built into the outside wall of the room, it becomes a formal shoin reception room. Hounsai's father, Tantansai, built the Yushin when he reached the age of sixty in 1954 in order to be able to serve tea to foreign guests using tables and chairs.

Sotan's Konnichian is the smallest at one and three quarter mats. Sotan built it in 1646, perhaps imitating the one-and-one-half-mat room at Jurakutei Castle that Rikyu built on the occasion of his retirement. Accordingly, only grand masters over sixty are supposed to use this room for tea. Passing Kan'untei, another of Urasenke's shoin-style eight-mat rooms, one enters Ryuseiken, a six-mat room that once served to connect Kan'untei, Konnichian, and Yuin, as well as Totsutotsusai. With the guests to the left of the host instead of on the right, as is customary, this is a room where one must prepare tea in the reversed (*gyaku*) fashion. The room was built by Gengensai with a protruding wall and a shitajimado, a small opening on the bottom provided with bamboo lattice. Hounsai uses this room only once a year on the occasion of *joyagama*, or the last tea of the year, on the evening of December 31. Tea is served with long noodles, symbols of long life, and the charcoal fire is then extinguished during the ceremony, only to be rekindled again with new fire for the next morning's *obukucha* (good luck tea).

During the time he has served as iemoto, Hounsai has designed more than forty tea rooms and huts. Most incorporate the major features of tea architecture as it developed through history. There are large reception rooms, but there are also many four-and-one-half-mat and even smaller rooms. Many of his tea huts also feature Gengensai's Western-style arrangement of tables and chairs (*ryurei*). In his designs, Hounsai has emphasized perhaps most of all the harmony between the tea hut and the environment. "The site and construction of the tea room, . . everything . . . comes under close scrutiny," he wrote in 1984.[17] The tea hut has to be embedded in nature, thus bringing nature into the city. He continues Rikyu's wabi tradition in using only natural building materials and a rustic tokonoma post. His tokonoma decorations are calligraphy, following the tradition of Juko and Rikyu.

Hounsai explained the tea room in terms of the Japanese concept of empty space, or *ma*, which he calls a "usefully useless" thing that can teach us about the properties of space. The focal point in this ma space is the tokonoma: "There is a tendency these days to think of this ma as wasted space, . . However, inasmuch as this ma of the tokonoma is rich with meaning and potential, we should consider it a truly useful thing."[18] Hounsai is referring to the Taoist notion that the usefulness of an object may reside in the empty space it provides. For example, the usefulness of a bowl lies not in the configuration, that is, in its walls, but in the empty space it creates. This space enables it to contain and control something as fluid as water.

Many wabi and shoin tea huts come with a simple garden centered upon the roji. With its compactly arranged trees and shrubs and stepping stones, this moss-covered path is structured to enhance the feeling of gradual separation from the mundane world, that is, to free the mind from worldly concerns. It has a *chumon* (middle gate), which represents the gateway of mu (emptiness) and a water basin. The *Roji Seicha Kiyaku* (September 3, 1584), which bears the seal of Rikyu, contains the following poem alleged to have been composed by Rikyu:

> The roji is merely
> A path leading away
> From the mundane world,
> And a way to clear the heart
> Of the dust [of the world] [19]

In this poem, Rikyu likens the roji to the metaphor of the burning house that appears in the *Lotus Sutra*. In this metaphor, existence is described as a burning house from which the Buddha tempts his heedless children with promises of gifts.

João Rodrigues observed these paths as a typical feature of tea:

> Although usually situated near a mansion or house, the teahouse should be located in a solitary and quiet place. In the surrounding garden there are stepping-stones, a pool of water, and a privy which is intended more for decoration than for actual use. The garden path runs naturally between bushes and trees (mostly pines), transplanted there with such elegance that they appear to have sprung up naturally. [20]

For Hounsai, proceeding along the roji is a process of purification. He sees in the roji the principle of *sei* (purity) in tea. But it is not just the purification of the body: "Washing the hands and rinsing the mouth before entering the tea room not only cleanses the physical body, but also purifies the heart." [21] Hounsai compares the roji's water basin to the holy water at the entrance of a Catholic church, with which the faithful purify themselves. [22] In one of his articles on the subject of the roji path, Hounsai tells us the following story:

> When Rikyu was studying tea under Takeno Jo'o, the latter had him clean the roji. With considerable effort, Rikyu swept the path and carefully picked up the pine needles from the moss. Then he reported to Jo'o that all was now clean, but Jo'o, after having inspected the path, declared that the work was not yet finished. So Rikyu cleaned the path again and again until no speck of dust could be found, but he was unable to satisfy his teacher. He then scattered a few leaves from the trees, and sprinkled the garden and the stone path with water. Jo'o was at last satisfied. [23]

Although it should be clean, the roji must not be too artificial; the visitor should receive the impression that it is natural, belonging to the season and the larger natural order Another aspect of the roji and Jo'o's aesthetic taste is revealed in the following incident:

> Jo'o had invited Rikyu to his mountain retreat, and when Rikyu at last reached the retreat, he stopped for a while, taking a deep breath and cooling off. Finally, he started to make his way along the roji path toward the tea hut. Reaching the stone basin, what did he see but a single, big taro leaf covering the surface of the basin. Drops of dew glittered on the leaf's surface. The sight took Rikyu's breath away. The host had anticipated that having climbed up the mountain in the summer heat, his guest would enjoy some coolness, which is why he placed that leaf on the basin, sprinkling it with water to impart a sense of coolness. [24]

The fourteenth grand master Tantansai told this story to his son to prepare him to always act according to the needs of the moment, something that Rikyu expressed by the phrase: "the workings of the very moment" (*ima no ima no hataraki*).

Tea Utensils

Tea utensils are ritual implements and, as such, are preserved, boxed, and wrapped with extreme care. The choice of utensils in tea depends upon the nature of the particular tea ritual. When tea is meant to assert and confirm the social order, the host uses and displays utensils symbolic of his social prestige and political and economic power. When tea is meant to transform its participants through shared communication, the host selects utensils that befit his guests' position and taste. Hounsai maintains that tea utensils represent the host, his taste and personality, as well as the host's regard for his guests. The utensils speak on the host's behalf. For example, a host might write his own calligraphy or carve his own tea scoop as an expression of intimacy with his guests, or he might display old utensils to allow his guests to commune with the masters of bygone days.[1]

The display of fine utensils often constitutes the charm of a meeting. Hounsai wrote that the choice of utensils determines and sets the mood of the tea: "One of the first things that the host of a tea gathering must do in preparation for the gathering is to decide what combination of utensils he or she will use; that is, to think about the purpose of the tea gathering and nature of the guests, and, with those things in mind, decide upon the hanging scroll, powdered-tea container, tea bowl, and so forth."[2]

The choice of utensils is what makes a gathering unique. This is perhaps the reason why many tea people in the sixteenth century believed that tea could not be done unless one possessed the appropriate utensils, and why they have collected them so avidly over the centuries. Some of the collections grew so large that they constituted considerable personal wealth. The value of tea utensils was determined not only by supply and demand; the history of the utensil, who had made and used it, and the social and political prestige of its past owners added to its economic value. Unlike other ritual implements, which are usually discarded after a single use in Japan, tea utensils circulated in the economy as items of exchange. Tea utensils were more personal, however, than money. Owners gave their utensils personal names as if they were children. While preserving their character as ritual props, tea utensils also often functioned as an ontic extension of the owner—that is, owners displayed these utensils as personal substitutes. In this sense, tea utensils share the animistic quality of other Japanese ritual implements. The more utensils one owns, the greater one's personal extension and the greater one's prestige. This led to the practice among people with political ambitions of hunting for utensils and amassing large collections.

The Ashikaga shoguns are the first political leaders on record to have collected tea utensils and art objects for display. We must distinguish this practice of collecting art objects from the tradition dating back to the ninth century (mid-Nara period) of preserving objects not destined to be displayed or exhibited. The items stored in the imperial repository called Shosoin in Nara exemplify this tradition of preservation. The motivation behind the Ashikaga-period collections was also quite different from the importation of Chinese furniture and eating utensils for daily use during the Kamakura period. The Ashikaga built their collections at a time when Chinese tea utensils, paintings, and calligraphy became objects of aesthetic contemplation and signs of economic and political power. The attribution of considerable aesthetic, economic, and political value to Chinese tea utensils derived perhaps from the fact that these utensils had once been sacred ritual implements. But rather than treating the objects as if they were taboo by wrapping them when not in use, or by discarding them as dangerously polluted by the sacred, tea utensils became aesthetic objects valuable in their own right, and as such they were available to enter the system of economic exchange.

Shogunal collections also coincided with a time when, due to renewed relations between the shogunal government and Ming-dynasty China, precious Chinese art objects became available in Japan. The shogunal government allowed Zen temples to conduct this trade and the profits to be used for their upkeep. The so-called Tenryuji-bune (Tenryuji temple boats) that the first Ashikaga shogun Takauji (1305–58) had licensed in 1342 put Chinese coins into circulation in Japan and helped Japanese merchants grow into a distinct social class with its own values and culture.

The Ashikaga shoguns displayed these objects as part of their entertainment rituals. Since these rituals were loaded with political and social significance, the utensils exhibited at such occasions also assumed political and economic weight. If a utensil had been used only once by a shogun or a prominent daimyo, then that utensil might have become nationally recognized as precious. Use by political potentates was enough to heighten the value of any utensil. A collector was able to monopolize art and use its value in public display to further his political ambitions.

It is no surprise that political leaders became overly concerned about authenticity, considering the political and economic value people came to attribute to art objects. For this reason the Ashikaga collectors instituted a curator system, placing their collections under the supervision of experts. These experts, called doboshu, were supposed to be able to distinguish between authentic pieces and fakes and determine their value and manner of display. This discriminating skill (*monozuki*) later came to dominate tea culture.

As a public expression of shogunal power and taste, tea had become an important public ritual. Art objects began to be displayed in shogunal entertainments, and the presence of a fake or inferior work could incite scorn and even hostility. The high stakes of the tea ritual created the need for arbiters of taste to advise the shoguns and other political leaders in matters of taste. We must understand that a display of taste was also a show of political authority and its appreciation (or contemplation) was a sign of political subordination.

Noami (1397–1471) was a doboshu in charge of authenticating, cataloguing, restoring, and remounting Chinese paintings and appraising and repairing Chinese tea utensils (*karamono*). He was the son of Maiami, who had already served the shogun as doboshu. The *Kundaikan Socho Ki*,[3] a list of the objects in shogun Ashikaga Yoshimasa's collection, also records Noami as one of the great masters in the display of art objects. He probably authored the *Gyobutsu Gyoga Mokuroku*, a catalogue of the shogunal collection now at the Tokyo National Museum. Later tea masters traced themselves back to the accomplishments of such doboshu as Noami. According to the *Yamanoue Soji Ki*, "Noami was the most expert among the doboshu and wrote the names of the paintings in the shogunal collection."[4] Yamanoue Soji continues to report that, because others had given them new names, the famous paintings ended up having more than one name. Naming was one of the duties of collectors and owners.[5]

The doboshu determined not only the value of utensils, but also the way to display and appreciate them, an activity the Japanese called *furumai*. The doboshu did what many Heian-period aristocrats had done before, namely, keep records as reference and as precedent for the benefit of future family generations. Some of these doboshu transmitted their skills to their sons and grandsons, establishing family monopolies of professional expertise. Thus, Noami's son Geiami continued in his father's tradition and is credited with writing the *Kundaikan Socho Ki*, mentioned above. Soami, Noami's grandson, wrote an addendum to it, entitled *Okazarisho*.[6] According to the *Sen Rikyu Yuishogaki* Rikyu is believed to have descended from Sen'ami, inheriting from his grandfather, an artistic tradition he helped to perfect.[7]

Other notable doboshu were the flower experts Ritsuami and Bun'ami. They knew how to select appropriate flowers to decorate the shogunal reception rooms. Kan'ami and Zeami were experts in the Noh drama, and Zen'ami in garden design. Sen'ami, Rikyu's alleged ancestor, was charged with caring for and displaying incense, tea bowls, and scrolls. Although these doboshu were placed in the shoguns' entourage and were allowed to carry swords, their status was halfway between priest and layman, and they were not eligible to assume the status of a samurai.

Either directly or indirectly, the sixteenth-century fathers of tea acquired doboshu skills and became their artistic successors. They learned from the doboshu how to appraise and display tea utensils. For Takeno Jo'o, correct use of tea utensils was equally as important as collecting them. Jo'o wrote in his *Ten Instructions for the Practitioners of Tea*, "It goes without saying that you must carefully select all things one can see [in the tea room] according to what is good or bad. They must be of sufficient beauty to interest people and be worthy of a suki."[8] Emphasizing the social roles of tea utensils, he explains that the tea practitioner must have appropriate utensils that communicate between host and guest. This kind of thinking derives directly from the doboshu.

Later on in his *Instructions*, he writes more specifically about the training required to handle certain utensils: "To be able to judge the famous utensils handed down from the masters of the past, according to a tea saying, requires more than twenty years of training under an expert." Because this training was practical rather than theoretical it required long study to acquire the necessary expertise. The long investment in time may also reflect the dynamics of the family monopoly that had developed around these skills.

Despite the decline of the Ashikaga military government after the start of the Onin Wars in 1467, art objects scrutinized by the doboshu retained their value and were coveted by power-seeking daimyo. In his effort to replace the ineffectual Ashikaga shoguns, the daimyo Oda Nobunaga acquired famous tea utensils from the Ashikaga and other daimyo collections. This activity of collecting, which Nobunaga used as a means to assert political power, came to be called "hunting for famous utensils" (*meibutsugari*). Once his collection grew, Nobunaga needed the expertise of a doboshu. In order to gain Nobunaga's support, the city of Sakai offered him Sen Rikyu, perhaps the city's most skilled artist, together with a tea caddy named "Tsukumogami." Like the Ashikaga, Nobunaga exhibited his collection to the public during large-scale tea parties at temples such as Shokokuji and Myokakuji in Kyoto. In 1574, he forced the opening of the Shosoin, the imperial repository at the Todaiji in Nara, and took a piece of precious *ranjatai* incense from it, claiming that Ashikaga Yoshimasa had done the same. By using the incense as a symbol of power, Nobunaga was arrogantly usurping the imperial prerogative. People interpreted this act as a claim to national hegemony, thus indicating the symbolic value tea objects had assumed by that time.

In 1582, Akechi Mitsuhide, one of Nobunaga's generals, rebelled against Nobunaga and burned down the Honnoji temple in Kyoto, where Nobunaga was staying. To escape being burned alive, Nobunaga committed suicide. A number of the precious objects that Nobunaga had brought with him the previous day from his stronghold at Azuchi were reduced to ashes. Among them was a dipper stand with an orange-shaped mouth and a celadon tea bowl that once belonged to Juko. Rikyu had sold the bowl to a daimyo for one thousand *kan* (the equivalent of about ten thousand bushels of rice). Juko's tea-leaf jar was rescued from the fire and eventually passed on to Nobunaga's successor Toyotomi Hideyoshi.

Given the importance of utensils in tea, it comes as no surprise that Europeans often mention utensils in their records. The Portuguese Jesuit Luis de Almeida (1525–83) wrote the following about his visit to a rich Sakai merchant, who was also a Christian and went by his Christian name Sancho: "All these utensils are regarded as the jewels of Japan, much in the same way as we value rings, gems, and necklaces made of many costly rubies and diamonds."[9] And about the prices some of these utensils yielded, he had this to say: "The value of these things is not surprising, for here in Miyako there is a lord who possesses a small porcelain vessel, shaped like a small cup and used to pour in tea powder. It is worth thirty thousand crowns; I am not sure about the price they ascribe to it, but many princes would give ten thousand crowns to buy it."[10]

By "princes," Almeida was referring to the daimyo. The prices of tea utensils also surprised Alessandro Valignano (1539–1606), the Jesuit visitor:

> It is quite incredible how highly they esteem these utensils, which are of a certain kind that only the Japanese can recognize. Often they give three, four, or six thousand ducats or even more for one of these pots or for one of these bowls or tripods. The king of Bungo showed me a small porcelain jar which among us would have no other use save to put into a birdcage as a water container. But he had bought this for nine thousand taels, which is about fourteen thousand ducats, although in all truth I myself would not have given one or two farthings for it.[11]

Here "the king of Bungo" refers to the daimyo of the province of Bungo, corresponding roughly to present-day Oita Prefecture in Kyushu. When one reads João Rodrigues's observations on tea, one realizes that all Europeans were equally flabbergasted by the prices of tea utensils. He wrote, "Some earthenware utensils may be worth twenty thousand crowns—something which will appear as madness to other nations."[12] Rodrigues, however, explains this differently from his compatriots: "In keeping with their melancholy disposition and with the purpose for which they collect such things, the Japanese find such mystery in these cha utensils that they attribute to them the value and esteem that other people place in precious stones and gems."[13] He sees the discernment and connoisseurship called suki behind this mystery. "Nature," he writes, "has endowed things with an elegance and grace which move the beholder to a feeling of loneliness and nostalgia, and a discernment of these qualities constitutes one of the main features of suki."[14]

From such European records, we discover the vastly differing values attributed to things by different cultures. Like Almeida, Valignano also pointed out the connoisseurship the Japanese have developed to judge the value of tea utensils: "And the Japanese have such understanding in these matters that they will immediately recognize the valuable pieces among a thousand similar utensils, just as European silversmiths can recognize and distinguish between false and genuine jewels."[15] He concludes, "It seems that nobody from Europe can ever reach this understanding because, however much we examine these things, we cannot determine what constitutes the value and distinctions between objects."[16] With the exception of Rodrigues and Valignano, most European observers were unable to understand the values the Japanese found in these utensils; Europeans looked at these things only from the point of view of the prices they yielded, but not as valuable art and ritual implements.

The extraordinary monetary value attributed to tea utensils is probably why Hideyoshi ordered all earthenware vessels called "Rusontsubo" (Philippine jars) to be sold to his commercial agent in Nagasaki. Francesco Carletti, a Florentine merchant who came to Japan in 1597, remarked about these jars, "Who ever would believe it?... Those cases are often worth five, six, or ten thousand *scudos* each, though ordinarily one would not say that they were worth a *giulo*, and the reason is that they have the property of preserving unspoiled—for nine, ten, and twenty years—a certain leaf they call cha."[17]

In the eyes of their beholders, tea utensils had a soul, which explains the reluctance of their owners to sell or give them away or, in later periods, to donate them to museums. Museum display, in particular, unrobed the utensils of their personality and their ability to represent their owner's self, hence the tendency of many collectors to hide their collections and display only appropriate pieces on important occasions to special guests.

Perhaps because of their low status as merchants, the Sakai tea amateurs preferred Japanese utensils (*wamono*) over the Chinese ones. Japanese utensils came to be closely associated with the wabi aesthetic. In the sixteenth century, when wabi became popular, Japanese craftsmen did not yet have the skills to match the standards of perfection and excellence of Chinese art. Nor was there a demand to compete artistically with China, because Japanese utensils were only regarded for their practical value, not as works of art. Hence, Japanese utensils were crude, simple, and poor looking. Yet, as the wabi aesthetic took hold, the wabi people discovered in these crude Japanese utensils an artistic quality and depth that was in keeping with wabi principles. As a result, Japanese utensils came to be esteemed so much that Shinshosai Shunkei, a tea man of Sakai, wrote in 1564, "The suki of these days no longer needs Chinese utensils. For a beginner or a wabi tea man even the charcoal and tea procedures are difficult; how much more difficult it must be for a wabi tea man to do without Chinese utensils. But, this too, can become an interesting [new] custom."[18]

Rikyu inherited taste and discrimination from his Sakai predecessors and advocated the use of unpretentious utensils in his wabi tea. Such utensils do not draw the attention of the guests away from themselves and each other. For Rikyu, uten-sils should create harmony rather than separate host and guest. In time, however, Japanese tea utensils assumed a value equal to Chinese utensils. João Rodrigues observed that wabi no longer represented poverty but "a wealthy poverty and an impoverished wealth, because the things used therein are poor in appearance but rich in price." [19]

Perhaps it was the high value of utensils that inclined some tea masters to advo-cate a tea without expensive objects. Kobori Enshu wrote on this subject:

> Do not depend on rare utensils. There is no difference between famous utensils and new ones. Even old utensils had once been new. Only uten-sils kept by families for a long time are eligible to be called famous ones. Don't use badly shaped utensils just because they are old and don't discard good-looking new ones. Don't seek too many and don't regret at having too few. To have but one utensil and use it repeatedly and hand it down to your children and grandchildren, this, too, is the Way. [20]

In his writings, Hounsai echoes his predecessors' advice and discourages the use of utensils simply because they are famous or old.

> Many fine, rare tea bowls with long, richly documented histories often come to my attention. Certain of these bowls strike me with their ugliness and I am dismayed with the way they have become so musty and old. Over the centuries tea grime has accumulated on the tea bowl and something like a heavy shroud conceals the tea bowl's beauty. Fame is of little conse-quence in this case. On the other hand, there are clean, well-cared-for utensils that are permeated with tea and grow more precious each time they are used. These utensils, filled with the spirit of tea, are truly beyond compare in their magnificence.

Hounsai adds that he finds the same to be true for tea practitioners. [21]

According to Hounsai, present-day tea practitioners are too eager to display famous utensils regardless of whether they fit the occasion or not. What is impor-tant, he maintains, is not their fame and value, but whether they match each other, the environment, the seasons, and of course the guests. [22]

CALLIGRAPHY

Hounsai echoes Rikyu in attributing to calligraphy a central position among the utensils of tea. Calligraphy is also a kind of "tea object." Calligraphy began playing an important role in tea when Murata Juko displayed the calligraphy the monk Ikkyu had given him. This custom goes back to the Song dynasty in China, when Zen monks used calligraphy to transmit the wisdom of past masters. Though Zen

placed great importance on a nonverbal "mind-to-mind" transmission, in time it became customary for the master to transmit a written record of his wisdom to the student when he felt that the student had gained enlightenment. Displaying such messages together with flowers, candles, and incense developed into a form of reverence and commemoration of the masters of old. The custom of displaying the calligraphy of Zen masters (known as *bokuseki)* was imported into Japan at the same time as both Zen and tea practice. Japanese Zen temples imitated the Chinese style of displaying calligraphy during memorial services. When Japanese monks traveled to China in an effort to receive the teachings of the masters, the masters would often write them something to take back to Japan, and there are many examples of such calligraphy still in the possession of Japanese Zen temples.

When tea became popular in Japan during the Kamakura period, it was practiced as an integral part of Chinese and Buddhist culture. The first calligraphic scrolls displayed at tea gatherings were therefore of Chinese provenance. When tokonoma were incorporated into shoin architecture in the Ashikaga period, Chinese calligraphy continued to dominate. The *Kundaikan Socho Ki* contains details about Chinese paintings and tea utensils, but it fails to mention anything about calligraphy. At that time, calligraphy still seems to have been confined to Zen temples and had not yet entered the reception rooms. It was only under Murata Juko's rapprochement of tea and Zen, temple procedures and tea procedures, that calligraphy came to be displayed in tea gatherings. As we have seen, the monk Ikkyu gave his disciple Juko a calligraphy by Yuanwu that, according to the *Yamanoue Soji Ki,* was displayed for the first time in a tea room. Tea masters such as Juko and the Sakai tea people such as Jo'o and Rikyu, who studied tea and Zen at Sakai's Zen temple Nanshuji or at Ikkyu's Daitokuji in Kyoto, also continued the tradition. *Tennojiya Kaiki,*[23] the tea record of Tsuda Sotatsu, a wealthy Sakai merchant, mentions some 430 tea gatherings between 1548 and 1566. Calligraphy is mentioned for about sixty of these gatherings; about one hundred gatherings do not list calligraphy, and the rest do not list a tokonoma decoration at all. All the calligraphy recorded was by Chinese masters, such as Xutang Zhiwu (1185–1269), Yuanwu Keqin (dates unknown), and Liaoan (also Nantang) Qingyu (1288–1363). Noteworthy is the usage of Japanese calligraphy by Shuho Myocho (also known as Daito Kokushi, 1282–1337), Shunrin Soshuku, the ninety-eighth head of Daitokuji, as well as by Fujiwara no Teika and Sanjonishi Sanetaka. According to the *Tsuda Sogyu Chanoyu Nikki,*[24] a record of tea gatherings hosted by Tsuda Sogyu, the successor of the Tennojiya shop in Sakai, from 1565 to 1585 reveals that paintings were used 145 times and calligraphy 150 times. The record of the Matsuya family's tea gatherings, *Matsuya Kaiki,*[25] is divided into three sections covering the years 1534 and 1596, 1586 to 1626, and 1626 to 1650. During this period, the display of paintings became the exception and calligraphy the rule.

Calligraphic work by the Chinese calligrapher and Zen monk Mian Xianjie (Jp., Mittan Kanketsu), now a national treasure, was first displayed in December 1574, when Tsuda Sogyu saw it. Next it appears in September 1577, at a tea party hosted by Yamanoue Soji. Then in October 1581 Sogyu himself displayed it. Sometime during the time Soji owned this calligraphy he asked Rikyu to remount it.[26] After Sogyu, the work changed hands until it ended up in the collection of Daitokuji monk Kogetsu Sogan, who displayed it in its Rikyu mounting at a tea party of June 1641 at Ryokoin subtemple. When Kobori Enshu built the Mittan teahouse in the Ryokoin, he built a tokonoma especially for this scroll and named the teahouse after its author. This episode demonstrates the centrality of calligraphy in tea. The scroll survives today as an example of Rikyu's taste in mounting scrolls in a way that enhances the calligraphy and not the surrounding material.

Although I have often used the verb "display" in the foregoing account, Rikyu warned of displaying utensils to impress the guests. One must put such implements in the service of nonself (*muga*). The host must not put his own ego on display; rather he must allow the objects he selects to unite host and guest. As stated in the *Nanboroku*, "There is no utensil more important than the hanging scroll. It is the way to achieve one mind between host and guest and leads to enlightenment. Among the hanging scrolls, calligraphy is number one."[27]

In wabi tea, which aimed at uniting tea and Zen, tea masters were reluctant to display objects that would suppress the individuality and creative ability of the viewers. They preferred objects of subdued beauty that could grow on the minds of the viewers, forcing them to look at them through their own hearts, conforming to the Buddhist teaching that there is no Buddhahood outside of one's own mind. These objects existed in the tokonoma for their own sake, rather than as the host's precious possessions. It was perhaps for this reason that once, when Rikyu invited Hideyoshi to an early morning party, he displayed a morning glory in the tokonoma rather than a scroll or a famous object of art. This selection of a delicate flower conveyed the message that it was appropriate to display things other than famous utensils in the tokonoma. Also, when the guest bows before the tokonoma scroll, it is not only in respect for the calligrapher, but also in deference to the message and its wisdom. Therefore, even Hounsai bows before his own calligraphy.

Having thus outlined the history of tea utensils and calligraphy, let us return to Hounsai and find out how much he inherited from these traditions and what his preferences are. As we have seen, he is fond of the Zen sayings "*Muhinshu*" and "*Honrai Muichibutsu*"; another Zen phrase he favors and likes to write in his calligraphy is "*Buji Kore Kinin*" (All Guests Are Main Guests). This comes from a Zen parable included in the *Rinzai Roku* (Record of Linji), and means that a person free of obstruction is on the path toward enlightenment. Being busy or otherwise drawn away from ourselves by exterior circumstances and obligations makes us forget about ourselves. This parable teaches us to always find our way back to ourselves, to the safety of our Buddha nature.

Hounsai also favors the phrase *"Bussho ni Nanboku Nashi"* (Buddha Nature Has No North Nor South). Another phrase, *"Hibi Kore Kojitsu"* (Every Day Is a Good Day) has a distinctly egalitarian message, because all humans share the will to make every day a good day. "It refers to the fact," he writes, "that the present is all there is and encourages the reader to accept the commonplace."[28] Another of Hounsai's favorite sayings is *"Kissa Ko,"* meaning "Just Have a Cup of Tea!" This comes from a Zen parable about the monk Zhaozhou Wuzi. One day, the story goes, a monk came to visit Zhaozhu. Zhaozhu asked him: "Have you been here before?" The monk replies, "Yes, I have." "Then have a cup of tea!" said Zhaozhu. Then another monk came. Zhaozhu asked him: "Have you been here before?" "No," he said. "Then have a cup of tea!" said Zhaozhu. Whoever you are, it does not matter, just have a cup of tea. According to Hounsai, this means that all people, regardless of where they come from, regardless of who they are, must drink a cup of tea.[29]

Perhaps his favorite calligraphy is the four characters: *Wa, Kei, Sei,* and *Jaku,* meaning harmony, respect, purity, and tranquility. These four principles of tea were set forth by Rikyu, who adapted them slightly from Murata Juko's *Kin, Kei, Sei,* and *Jaku* (humility, respect, purity, and tranquility). According to Hounsai, these are the four basic principles governing both procedures and human relations in tea. For him, these represent "tea's highest ideals."

Harmony reflects "both the evanescence of all things and the unchanging in the changing." Harmony means "not pretending," "walking the path of moderation," and "never forgetting the attitude of humility." Respect is the sincerity that opens our hearts to our fellow humans and to our environment. It recognizes "the dignity of each." Purity not only means sweeping the tatami mats or the roji path, but as it does in Shinto and Buddhist ritual, purifying both body and mind at the same time. It is as much spiritual as it is physical. "The act of cleansing thus enables one to sense the pure and sacred essence of things, man, and nature." Finally, tranquility is the result of practicing the first three principles. Hounsai explains this concept as a paradox: "That we can find a lasting tranquility within our own selves in the company of others."[30]

Hounsai likes his calligraphic messages to represent the seasons. In an essay entitled "An Art of the Seasons," Hounsai wrote, "In summer . . . scrolls that speak of wind and water are often hung."[31] One of his favorites for spring is "Petals of the Plum Tree Floating on the Water" (*Toka Ryusui*). This comes from the Chinese poem:

> *I ask myself: Why is it that I live in these green mountains?*
> *I laugh and find no answer, but my heart is at peace with itself;*
> *The peach petals float on the water and are carried far, far away;*

> *This is not the human world, but a world apart, the world of pure nature.* [32]

This calligraphy best suits the month of March, especially the "Peach Festival" of March 3 (Momo no Sekku), a time to pray for good health and longevity. March is also the time when, every fifty years, the Senke families hold special services for Rikyu. Hounsai likes to display the calligraphy *"Shujinko,"* which I will quote in full in Hounsai's biography. Another calligraphy one may encounter at Rikyu's memorial services is *"Hyakuhyaku Sensen Manmannen,"* meaning "One Hundred One Hundred, One Thousand One Thousand, Ten Thousand Ten Thousand Years," a kind of prayer that Rikyu's tea may endure forever.

One of the themes of May is "The Fragrant Wind That Comes from the South Delicately Cools the Pavilion" (*Kunpu Ji Nanrai Denkaku Biryo o Shozu*). This is the time of year when the wind carries the fragrance of the young leaves.

"Blue Mountains and Green Water" (*Seizan Ryokusui*), a calligraphy appropriate for spring, comes from the famous Chinese poem:

> *The river is green and the birds more and more white,*
> *The mountains are blue and the flowers about to burn,*
> *Again, this spring passes in front of my eyes.*
> *Which day of which year will it be, when I can return home?* [33]

At September tea meetings, Hounsai often displays "The Pure Wind Wipes Off the Moon at Dawn" (*Seifu Akatsuki o Harau*), which originated in Song-dynasty China. This reminds one of the start of autumn, when a pure, cool wind blows as if to cleanse the face of the moon at dawn.

In the words of Hounsai, the hanging scroll is the most important tea implement "because the hanging scroll directly reveals the theme of the gathering." He elaborates on the importance of the hanging scroll, writing, "For example, if the gathering is to commemorate a happy event, an appropriate one-line calligraphic work, piece of Japanese poetry, or other such work is selected, and the kettle, tea bowl, tea scoop, and other items are in turn chosen in accordance with the chosen scroll." [34] In this way, Hounsai echoes Rikyu's philosophy of calligraphy as recorded in the *Nanboroku*, where he writes that calligraphy makes us mindful of the wisdom and the Buddhist teachings of the great Zen patriarchs which, according to him, are highly important in the Way of Tea.

Tea Procedures

K now-how, procedures, and protocol (etiquette) are essential features of all ritual. To be able to participate in ritual, one must know its procedures, the ritual "grammar" or "culture." Tea is just such a ritual, with a varied and complex set of procedures. There are presently over two hundred procedures, more than a single individual can master.

Like tea utensils, tea procedures mirror the host's "heart" and the larger philosophical aims of the tea. They symbolize universal order and harmonious human relations. Like drama, tea produces what Hounsai calls a catharsis.[1]

Tea procedures have sometimes been compared to a drama and the tea room to a stage. In Hounsai's opinion, however, such a definition is only acceptable with the following reservations:

> Unlike the typical stage arts such as Noh or Kabuki, where there is a director-performer, and a passive audience of onlookers, the tea drama involves active participation by the host and guest alike. The guest himself sits upon the stage which the host sets, and reading the subtle cues sent out by the host, the guest plays his own part in the totality of the production. The host provides the props, controls the sound and lighting effects, to which the guest's mood responds, and shared between them, each has a perfect singular moment.[2]

Like traditional Japanese drama, tea is accompanied by a rhythm that Hounsai compares to dance. Tea must respond to the rhythms of *jo* (slow), *ha* (intermediate), and *kyu* (fast) that characterize classical Japanese music and dance. "What gives them [tea procedures] beauty is their quality and timing," wrote Hounsai in 1981. Hounsai calls this "temporal space," and says that unless one pays due attention to its properties and rhythmical requirements, there will be "discord, distorted actions, and irregular rhythms."[3] Thus tea is bound to an interior rhythm, a rhythm that corresponds to the season of the year.

Tea procedures respond most of all to the seasons. "A tea room and the things that are briefly placed in it should always mirror the natural world of its surroundings, enhancing the particular season rather than competing with it," writes Hounsai. "Men of tea have always tried to live within the framework of the changing seasons."[4] To impart a sense of the seasons is an essential function of tea. As a ritual, it must fit in the larger cosmic order. A seasonless tea is impossible.

Yet, it was not tea that invented the seasons as a cultural category. This system of categorization was used much, much earlier in Japanese court poetry. The earliest collection of court poetry, the *Kokinshu* of 905, categorized the poems by the seasons, and a poem was not satisfactory unless it referred to the season in which it was composed. Likewise, tea devotees must have utensils befitting each season. Eventually, this was incorporated into other arts such as, for example, textile design. A courtesan would never wear a summer kimono in winter, and vice versa. This need for seasonal reference is the reason why women had to have at least four kimono, each with the appropriate seasonal patterns and design. Room decorations, flowers, and of course food—all had to convey an unmistakable seasonal message. As for tea, someone once asked Rikyu, "What is the secret of tea?" Rikyu answered, "Prepare tea so that it tastes good, place the charcoal so that it heats the water, arrange the flowers as they are [in nature] and, in the summer, impart a sense of coolness, and in the winter, a sense of warmth. There are no other secrets."[5]

When he said this, Rikyu was perhaps referring to a tea party to which his teacher Jo'o had once invited him. Jo'o had placed a wet taro leaf on the water basin that stood along the roji path. The leaf itself does not produce coolness, of course, but it imparts to the viewer a pronounced sense of coolness. The rest is spiritual; the guest must overcome heat with his own mental effort. He or she must "become" the heat or cold, as must the host who, on hot summer days, must sit in front of a burning brazier and make tea. Overcoming heat requires spiritual strength.

Hounsai selects from his utensils those that are most appropriate to the season. In the summer, the host will use flatter, thinner tea bowls, whereas in the winter he uses thicker, more rounded ones to impart a sense of warmth. Even the water jars may change according to the season. In summer, Hounsai sometimes uses glass or crystal jars to create an atmosphere of coolness. During the Tanabata festival of July 7, Hounsai places a large fig leaf on his water jar instead of a lid.

The tea room setting also changes depending on the season. In the winter, tea is made in a sunken hearth that can occupy one or two places in the room, depending on the architecture of the tea hut. In spring the tea kettle hangs on a chain attached to the ceiling above the sunken hearth. In the summer, the hearth is closed and a brazier, used to heat the water, is placed on a predetermined spot (the temaeza) in the room. The host may also be forced by the teahouse architecture to use reverse (*gyaku*) procedures, in which he folds the silk cloth used for the purification of utensils at the right rather than, as is usual, at the left side of his body. In this procedure, the water jar and waste-water receptacle are placed on the right rather than on the left side of the host. The tea setting and procedures will also change in accord with the time of day. Tea gatherings called *asa chaji* (morning tea) take place at dawn or early in the morning; *shogo chaji* (noon tea) takes place at noon and early afternoon; and *yobanashi* (night talk) takes place at night, illuminated by candlelight. Asa chaji is usually held in summer, to enjoy the cool of the early morning.

Tea proceedings also change depending upon whether thin tea or thick tea is being served. In thin tea, each guest receives his or her own cup, but when thick tea is served, guests share the same bowl. After use, each guest must clean the rim before handing the bowl to the next guest. In thick tea, the host must measure the amount of tea so that all guests have their three sips. In addition to these, there are two charcoal procedures (*sumidemae*) for rekindling the fire in the winter hearth (shozumi) or in the summer brazier (*gozumi*). After thick tea has been served, the host must replenish the charcoal fire, and only then is he able to prepare and serve a separate cup of thin tea for each of the guests. Hounsai teaches that training in these procedures requires time and selfless discipline.

Even the quality of the water may change tea procedures. In the so-called "famous water procedure," or *meisuidate*, water from an especially famous source is placed in a wooden bucket surrounded by white paper strips indicating the sacredness of the water. The main guest must ask the host to explain the provenance of the special water to all the guests. Japan has many famous sources of water. One of these, Ochanomizu (Tea Water), became the name of an area in Tokyo. Another is the Minase River, the location of the first Suntory brewery. There are many more such tea water sources, whose identification in a tea setting impresses the guests.

Finally there are various outdoor procedures, including the table-and-chair ryurei or *misonodana* procedures that were first introduced to accommodate non-Japanese.

Despite the numerous tea diaries written by tea devotees beginning in the sixteenth century, we do not know exactly how Juko, Jo'o, or Rikyu served tea. We know what utensils they used in what setting, but the step-by-step procedures are not on record. It would be a mistake to presume that the iemoto system has preserved the exact form of tea from Rikyu's time to the present. As I have argued previously, tea masters had to adapt tea to the new social fabric of the Tokugawa and the subsequent Meiji period. The degree to which they preserved Rikyu's tea is therefore a complex problem. Also, each iemoto had to make minor adjustments to satisfy guests and patrons of the noble and the merchant classes, and, in time, foreign visitors to Japan. The timing or rhythm of the tea ceremony must also have changed from generation to generation. As experts have discovered recently, the rhythm of Noh plays has slowed down markedly since the fifteenth and sixteenth centuries; Hounsai has responded to this trend with his encouragement to proceed expeditiously. Each generation comes with its own tempo and tea had to adapt itself to these rhythms.

Despite the fact that later generations of tea masters tried to preserve Rikyu's tradition, or what they believed to be Rikyu's tea legacy, Rikyu himself, in typical wabi spirit, de-emphasized procedures. For him, tea procedure was not the most important thing in tea. We learn this from the following episode:

> Sen no Rikyu was once invited by a tea grower and merchant of Uji. He arrived at the merchant's house at the appointed day with some followers. Although the merchant had invited Rikyu, he doubted whether he would be able to come up to the standards of such a great master as Rikyu. The excitement and pleasure of having Rikyu as his guest prevented him from preparing tea in a tranquil state of mind. During his preparation, his hand hit the tea scoop, making it fall from the top of the tea caddy, and causing the tea whisk to fall over as well. While Rikyu's followers laughed at the merchant's ineptitude, Rikyu was pleased and said: "This is the best tea I ever experienced!"

On his way back home, the followers asked Rikyu why he praised such ineptness, saying that it was the best tea he had ever experienced. Rikyu replied that this man did not invite him with the intention of showing off his skills. "He simply wanted to serve me tea with his whole heart. . . . He devoted himself completely to making tea for me, not worrying about making errors. His sincerity impressed me."[6]

Hounsai often says that tea procedures are ultimately only a means to free the student from the rules. One learns these procedures not for their own sake but to attain the highest freedom of expression. This indicates how much tea procedures and the process of mastering them were indebted to Zen training.

Under the title "Adaptation in Tea," Jakuan quotes from the *Nanboroku* to clarify his view of Zen and tea procedures: "The transmission from master to pupil as to how to place the utensils and to prepare tea includes many details, and one cannot avoid them. But once one has mastered them all, from the basic rules to the secrets of yin and yang, one is free to apply unlimited variations. Variation means overstepping the regulations while observing them."[7] Jakuan explains that if one consciously oversteps the regulations, it is no longer the Way of Tea, and that it is only acceptable if one does it naturally, without thinking and after having thoroughly mastered the rules.

Like Zen training, Hounsai wrote, tea practice has three parts: *do* (path), *gaku* (knowledge), and *jitsu* (practice). These three aspects must be mastered to become a perfect host or guest.[8] Through practice, the tea student must acquire deep knowledge, not just about tea but also about life. What enables the student to accomplish this is the Way of Tea, that is, tea practice as a way of life, a total and selfless commitment. "Gradually, after many repetitions, it seems almost as though the procedure performs itself and it becomes as natural as walking," wrote Hounsai.[9] Tea is no longer procedures; "for me," he continues, "tea is using my mind and other resources to discover my own attitude toward life."[10] It is only after having reached this stage of skill that one is able to express oneself through tea.

Offertory tea is a tea procedure that only the grand tea master can perform. When offered to a Shinto shrine it is called kencha, and when it is presented to the altar of a Buddhist temple it is called kucha. Both procedures follow the regular *shin no shin daisu*, the most elevated procedure in tea. Special features of this procedure include the grand master clapping his hands as if to summon the deity as he stands before the daisu table before making the offering tea; and lifting up the tea bowl resting on a tray, as is done in Chinese-style proceedings. When the grand master presents thick tea he uses a white silk cloth (fukusa), whereas when serving thin tea he uses a purple cloth. In the case of thick tea, he rinses the tea whisk while carrying the tea bowl in his hand; in thin tea, he does this while the tea bowl rests on the floor. Before he lowers the tea caddy from the top shelf of the table, called the ten ita (heaven board), he rubs his hands as an act of purification. Before he pours tea powder into the bowl, he puts on a white mask to prevent his breath from polluting the sacred tea. It is important that the offertory tea be presented with a pure heart. The ceremonies of kencha and kucha are public displays of the iemoto's authority. Mistakes must therefore be avoided at all cost. It is interesting to observe that for tea ceremonies when the host offers tea to important guests (*kinin*), he uses similar procedures, suggesting that he treats special guests almost as if they were living deities.

Tea Food

In matters of food, Hounsai remained particularly attached to the traditions transmitted to him from the sixteenth and seventeenth centuries, the most formative centuries in tea. Since Hounsai's approach to food is so influenced by his predecessors, we must trace the history of tea food from the sixteenth century up to Hounsai. Thanks to the detailed records past tea men have kept about their tea meetings and food, there is much detailed information available.

From the *Miyoshitei Onari no Ki* of the Tokugawa period, we learn that in formal banquets, Ashikaga shoguns included as many as seven trays of food (*shichigosan*). This banquet would be followed, in a separate room, by three servings of saké and snacks (*nijusankon*), which lasted until early the next morning. A typical banquet, to conclude from this source, lasted about twelve hours and included Noh, Kyogen, and a traditional dance form called Shirabyoshi.[1]

Wabi food, the rules of which had already been set by Rikyu's predecessor Jo'o, considerably abbreviated and simplified these formal banquets of the shoin reception rooms. In his *Jo'o's Instructions for his Disciples*, Jo'o is said to have pointed out that "Even if one has special guests, serving more than three dishes and one soup is inappropriate to tea."[2] The meal, he said, should be a simple one, as it was served in Zen temples. The *Nanboroku* states, "The meal served in the small room should consist of only one soup and two or three side dishes and saké should be offered sparingly. Elaborate food does not belong in a wabi room."[3]

Wabi-style food was nothing new; it was a revival of Zen food commonly called *kaiseki*, a reference to the heated stones which monks bound around their stomachs to prevent hunger during their long hours of meditation. Kaiseki food therefore meant a simple, frugal meal not intended to fill one's stomach but is, as Rikyu said, "barely enough to prevent you from starving." Like wabi tea, kaiseki strove to limit the number of dishes to a bare minimum and to serve them in containers suited to the food and the seasons. Beyond its nutritional functions, wabi-style food was designed to instill among the guests a feeling of austerity, of "barely enough," but also to lead them, through a beautifully prepared and arranged meal, to a realization of the profound beauty of simplicity. Hounsai explains that food in tea ritual is a kind of spiritual communication between the host and his guests. Similar to the choice of utensils, the selection of foods communicates the host's "heart."

Hounsai tells us the following story that sums up the essence of wabi food.

> One snowy winter morning, so the story goes, Doan invited his father Rikyu to attend a snow-viewing tea party. Although the weather was dreadful, Rikyu determined to go. When Rikyu arrived at his son's house, he saw something dark moving about in the snow-covered vegetable patch in the back. It was his son wearing a straw raincoat and a sedge hat, digging out vegetables in the garden. Obviously, Doan had been gathering vegetables for the tea party. Rikyu was looking forward to the pleasant dish using these simple, winter vegetables. During the party, however, when Rikyu lifted the lid of the soup bowl, he found to his surprise that the bowl contained sea bass and some greens, but not the vegetables he was expecting. Sea bass in winter was out of season, scarce, and expensive. The disappointed Rikyu reprimanded his son, saying that rare delicacies have no place in wabi tea, which required only simple, seasonal, and everyday ingredients. For Rikyu, any tea served in a wabi environment had to be served in the wabi style, including the food preceding the tea.[4]

For wabi food one should only use seasonal vegetables and fish and, if possible, only what one has on hand. Elaborate food brought from distant places and acquired at high cost does not belong in wabi tea: "They need not be delicacies, and they need not be rare. It is the human quality behind their serving that is to be appreciated," writes Hounsai.[5] In the following episode, we learn even more about Rikyu's tea-food preferences:

> In Moriguchi [between Kyoto and Osaka], there lived a wabi man Rikyu knew, and Rikyu promised to pay him a visit and have tea with him one day. It was winter. Rikyu was returning to Kyoto from Osaka when he remembered this man and he decided to pay him a visit. Though it was late at night when he arrived, the man greeted him heartily and guided Rikyu into his home. His dwelling was truly in the wabi style and appealed to Rikyu. After a while, Rikyu saw beyond the window a man in the garden. It was the host, who came out with a bamboo pole and was knocking down some lemons. He laid down the pole and came back in carrying two lemons. As Rikyu was watching this, he thought: "He will surely serve me

these lemons," and he was very much looking forward to the wabi meal. As he had expected, the host brought in a miso soup with lemon in it. After they had some saké, however, the host declared: "Something has just been delivered from Osaka," and brought in fish cake, saying, "Yesterday evening I ordered something we can eat with the saké. This is something very special." This broke the spell and, while there was still some saké left, Rikyu said, "I have urgent business in Kyoto and must leave." The host tried everything to keep Rikyu, but without avail. Rikyu left for Kyoto. The reason was that the host had served something not befitting wabi tea.[6]

Kusumi Soan (1636–1728), who recorded this story, adds, "Although one serves various things, in wabi one should not serve things that do not go together."

A similar story tells of one Hiki Hyakuo who invited Rikyu in the summer and served him watermelon sprinkled with sugar, a rare and expensive commodity at that time. Rikyu only ate the parts where there was no sugar, saying that melons have their own sweetness.[7]

Because Rikyu's wabi food set the precedent for Hounsai's servings, let us look into the records of tea food to find out in greater detail what kinds of food tea people served before and during Rikyu's time. The earliest record of food served at a tea meeting comes from the *Matsuya Kaiki*. Under the date of September 12, 1537, the record reveals that individual trays were brought in to the guests. In the front section of the tray there was a bowl of rice and a bowl of soup with greens, and in the back section, grilled salmon and shellfish with the shell attached. A separate serving of freshwater herring was offered in the *hikimono* fashion of passing a food tray from guest to guest. After this came three varieties of dessert. This was an abbreviated version of the first tray in *honzen*, or formal meals.

By the middle of the sixteenth century, when wabi became popular, many tea devotees abided by the principle of *ichiju sansai*, meaning one soup and three side dishes, which Jo'o had recommended. This is also what João Rodrigues observed: "The host disappears into the house, and then, beginning with the senior guest, places in front of each one small tables on which are neatly arranged rice, vegetables, and a dish of some prized fish or bird. The host then retires again into his house, leaving the guests to eat in silence; from time to time reappearing to see if they desire more to eat. . . . Then he clears away the tables, serves some fruit as dessert, and then retires from the scene."[8]

One notices in the histories of tea gatherings, however, a certain degree of freedom within these limits. Looking at the *Matsuya Kaiki*, we observe a number of variations. Among the twenty-eight tea meetings described in the *Matsuya Kaiki*, sixteen mention food. Among them, nine were light meals, such as noodle soup, dumplings, and a gelatinous sweet called *suisen* (made of *kuzu* or devil's tongue powder and cut into thin, noodle-like strips). Four meals consisted of one soup and three side dishes. In one gathering on April 12, 1533 at Kofukuji temple in Nara, noodles were served after tea and not, as was customary, before. This reminds one of the New Year tea parties Hounsai hosts, during which tea comes first and food and saké after.

At the gathering at Kofukuji, for example, there was a dish of salted fish and one of marinated freshwater salmon placed on a tray with rice and a soup. There was in addition broiled sweetfish served on a tray passed from guest to guest. This was followed by a soup of sea bass, making two soups and three side dishes in all. The dishes consisted mainly of marinated, boiled, and broiled foods, as well as liquid and solid foods.

Kaiseki food was served on a limited number of trays, setting it apart from the formal honzen dishes served on four-legged trays. The confined space of wabi tea huts and rooms prevented the serving of large amounts of food on numerous trays. Rikyu is known to have served only one side dish, but two soups on a number of occasions and, at least once, as many as five side dishes, sometimes presented in two servings on two separate trays. According to the *Rikyu Hyakkaiki*, between August 1590 and February 1591 he served "one soup, one side dish," "one soup, two side dishes," "one soup, three side dishes," "one soup, four side dishes," "one soup, five side dishes," "two side dishes and no soup," and "two soups and two side dishes." When hosting Toyotomi Hideyoshi, Rikyu used a second tray.

On February 27, 1544, according to the *Matsuya Kaiki*, Rikyu served rice, soup with tofu and wild horsetail, and three side dishes: gluten cakes, a vegetable called *udo*, and jellyfish. The sweets consisted of *kaya* nuts, chestnuts, and dried octopus (at this time, "dessert" was not necessarily restricted to sweet foods). By the middle of the sixteenth century, such three-course meals, including a final course, came to be served by particularly eager hosts. The *Matsuya Kaiki* documents one such gathering under the date March 12, 1555. The merchant host served rice, codfish soup, broiled salmon, and cuttlefish on the first tray and sea bream, a kind of shellfish called *akagai*, and chicken soup served on a low lacquered tray (*oshiki*) on the second tray. Then a wood tray with an arrangement of carp and a type of sea snail called *tsubetagai* was passed from guest to guest. In addition, there was a middle course with kuzu sweets and crabmeat and a final course with noodles and clams.

More elaborate foods were served, it seems, at exceptional occasions such as the opening of a new teahouse, the display of a new utensil, or a *kuchikiri*, the opening of a tea-storage jar. The latter occasioned Rikyu to invite a number of close friends and associates to a tea meal on the last day of October 1576. The food included a dish of dressed ingredients, broiled salmon, and a soup of wild goose and greens. After the tea, Rikyu offered another course consisting of a clear soup with blowfish. For May 23, 1581, the *Tennojiya Kaiki* records the serving of one soup and nine side dishes during the morning and, at lunch, an additional meal consisting of pounded rice (*mochi*), fish, clear soup, and various additional dishes. Boiled rice with hot water poured over it (*yuzuke no meshi*) was served in the evening. This was to commemorate the first use of a particular tea caddy.

When Hideyoshi was invited to tea, Rikyu would serve more than one meal. In a morning tea on September 13, 1590, Rikyu first brought each guest a short-legged, cedar tray on which he served rice, fermented bean (*natto*) soup, and marinated eels. On a second tray, he brought a soup of wild duck, a dish of dressed ingredients, and broiled sea bream. This amounted to two soups and three side dishes. At midday, when tea had been served, a luncheon consisting of rice in hot water, a vegetable soup, a dish of dressed ingredients, skewered abalone, and braised miso (*yakimiso*) served in a gilded bucket-shaped container was served in a large adjacent room. This was followed by a second tray with eel and steamed fish paste (*kamaboko*). Rikyu seems to have preferred to place rice, a soup, and one side dish on the main tray. This has remained a standard arrangement to this day.

After Rikyu, Furuta Oribe tended toward even simpler servings, in spite of his inclination toward serving the hierarchical daimyo tea. According to the *Furuta Oribe no Sho Dono Kikigaki*, he was reluctant to even serve two soups on two trays. On September 11, 1597, Oribe prepared a simple meal with one soup and two side dishes, a grilled citron served with rice and soup, and broiled eel and pickles brought in separately and served by passing from guest to guest. Oribe cooked the food himself. According to a work entitled *Furuta Oribe Chakaiki*, among thirty-four gatherings in which food is mentioned, Oribe served one soup and three side dishes in nineteen cases, and two soups and five side dishes on six occasions. On one occasion he served one soup and five side dishes, and, on another, one soup and two side dishes plus a last round with grated-taro rice and four side dishes.[9] Whereas Rikyu strove not to serve more than three side dishes, Oribe strove not to serve more than one soup.

After Rikyu's death, and as daimyo tea flourished, food became more elaborate. On July 2, 1634, Hosokawa Sansai invited a monk and a merchant to tea. He served an elaborate two-course meal with rice in a gold- and silver-speckled lacquer bowl; soup with *matsutake* mushrooms and potato; and a dish of *namasu*.[10] The second course consisted of *iwatake* lichen, *konyaku* (devil's tongue) jelly, and amaranthus with miso; and soup with *mozuku* seaweed. Grilled salmon trout, tofu with walnuts on top, sweet smelt sushi, shrimp, seaweed, and black peas were served by passing from guest to guest. There were also several desserts.

Kobori Enshu, however, continued to serve wabi-style foods, as we learn in a record of a tea gathering on February 24, 1599. Enshu's successor Sekishu also served light meals. We do not know the kinds of food served by Sotan, but one of his four famous disciples, Miyake Boyo, at a tea gathering on February 23, 1648, served rice, soup with greens, and shellfish in the shell; grilled sea bream and shaved, dried codfish passed from guest to guest; and just one dessert, consisting of mushrooms. On another occasion, on December 5, 1683, he served one soup and four side dishes.

During Rikyu's day, since there were only one or two side dishes, it is said that nothing was left uneaten. In later periods, however, when it became the fashion to serve more dishes, it was not necessary to eat everything. There was also the question of whether the guest must eat all food served, even those dishes that they dislike. An interesting story illustrates this problem. Toyotomi Hideyoshi held a tea party at which he served his guests the much-prized treat of sea-cucumber entrails. One of the guests strongly disliked the dish, but felt that if he did not eat it he would offend his host and fall out of favor. So he gulped it down without chewing it. Seeing this, Hideyoshi concluded that he must truly like the dish and ordered another one for him. The unfortunate man felt sick, but managed to last through the first half of the tea meeting. He could not, however, bring himself to reenter the tea room after the recess and, informing a fellow guest of his troubles, left and hurried home. Later tea men, therefore, relaxed the rules of eating everything and determined that all the food left on the tray untouched by chopsticks could be returned without giving insult. [11]

By the Genroku period (1688–1704), the economy had stabilized and, even among the Sen family, meals became increasingly elaborate. From the *Chanoyu Kondate Shinan* we learn: "In the old days, there was an age when, though they served quite unimpressive food such as brown rice, simple broths, and broiled salted sardines on a *yamaoshiki* [tray], people found it amusing and tea also enjoyed popularity, but now in our age, when people have developed extravagant tastes, they think poorly of tea that comes with the old kinds of food." [12] It was in the Genroku period that the food served in tea to this day was established.

In wabi-style tea gatherings, hosts usually served little saké, and then only with meals. This was to prevent drunkenness and uncontrolled behavior in tea rooms, as we learn from a text written in 1572: " Saké should not be drunk in quantity. When the host has taken great trouble and offered a bowl of his precious powdered tea, or when he has exhibited his private treasures; when old friends come together or when refined conversation is the object, drunkenness on the part of either the guest or host is rude and inconsiderate." [13] João Rodrigues also confirms this when he wrote, "Next he serves warm wine, bidding them to drink what they will but not pressing them to drink more." [14]

Hounsai likes to serve simple, natural meals. For him, a warm-hearted hospitality is the most important thing, far surpassing any rare delicacy. He wrote, "Such warm-hearted hospitality lies in such acts as the handpicking of fresh vegetables from one's snow-covered garden for guests one has invited on a snowy winter day, and offering a meal to those guests consisting of fresh, home-prepared dishes. They need not be delicacies, and they need not be rare. It is the human quality behind their serving that is to be appreciated." [15]

The kaiseki that has become the most common in recent times is the *ichiju nisai* format of one soup and two side dishes, which Hounsai also serves.

Given the time and effort a host would have to put into the preparation of tea food, most tea meetings today do not include food. Hounsai regrets that people practice tea without offering a full course. "I . . . notice," he writes, "that the *chaji* [full course] tends to be forgotten about in tea lessons; that the tendency is for people to undertake tea practice solely for the sake of just that—undertaking tea practice. . . . I think we should once again recognize that the things we learn and practice in the classroom are steps meant to lead to chaji." [16] Hounsai sees one reason behind this: the lack of utensils and fear of criticism. "What is important," he writes, "is not the utensils, but one's sincerity of heart." [17]

I cannot close this chapter without referring to the tea sweets that guests to a tea party today always enjoy. There are two kinds of sweets served in tea: the moist, soft *omogashi* (heavy sweet) that precedes thin tea and the hard *higashi* (dry sweet) that comes with thick tea. When there is no thick tea, higashi can also be served with thin tea. Both kinds tend to be very sweet, especially the higashi, which consists mainly of sugar. Such sweets only came to be served in tea, however, after the Portuguese discovered Japan in 1542 and brought refined sugar from Europe. What sweets did the tea hosts serve before that time? According to the *Matsuya Kaiki*, these were mainly nuts, such as chestnuts and gingko nuts, and fruits such as kumquats and persimmons. They also served a great variety of snacks made from cooked rice pounded into a glutinous mass and mixed with some special flavor, something the Japanese seemed to have learned from the Chinese. After the Portuguese arrived, a kind of sugar-based *konpeito* (from the Portuguese *confeito*) and *aruheito* (from *alfeloa*), prepared in various natural shapes, appeared in tea, another testimony of the highly eclectic nature of early Japanese tea.[18]

Tea Flowers

For Hounsai, tea flowers bring yet another seasonal reference into the tea room. Flowers do not simply decorate, they draw attention to the season and the cosmic order. Hounsai wrote that tea flowers remind us that we belong to nature and that our own lives, though intense, are quite fragile. Flowers also remind us of the "now," a now for its own sake that, in Hounsai's mind, is so important in tea.[1]

Like tea, flower arranging (ikebana) started as a Buddhist practice that the warriors adapted to their own lifestyle. It began with the custom of placing fresh flowers each morning on the Buddhist altar. Later this religious practice became an artistic pursuit among the monks of the Kyoto temple Rokkakudo. The monk Ikenobo Senkei (fifteenth century) was particularly skilled in this art, and his work became the basis for a school of flower arranging. The sculptural arrangements that made Senkei famous were quickly brought into the shogunal residences, where they were placed under the supervision of the doboshu. The art of arranging flowers was then taken up by the merchant class, and has continued to this day under the control of the iemoto of each school. Shoin tea, as much as wabi tea, drew upon the traditions of ikebana. Under the influence of wabi tea, however, the lavish styles of shoin arrangements were abandoned for more simplified forms. A good example of this trend is Rikyu's famous "morning glory tea party."

Hideyoshi, so the story goes, had heard of the beautiful morning glories blooming each morning along the hedge leading up to Rikyu's tea hut. Wishing to see them, he announced his visit. When he arrived, he was surprised to see that all the morning glory blossoms had been cut off, and not a single one was to be seen on the hedge. When the somewhat frustrated Hideyoshi entered the tea hut, however, he realized that Rikyu had placed a single morning glory in a bamboo vase. This convinced the flabbergasted warlord once more of Rikyu's artistic taste and depth.

Rikyu had preferred to present his host with one morning glory in the alcove, knowing it would make a much more powerful impact there than the multitude Hideyoshi would have seen blooming along the hedge. This preference for one over many is typical of the wabi aesthetic; in addition, the small is preferred over the big, little over much, the subdued over the extravagant, the evanescent over the permanent, and depth over superficiality. Tea flowers must represent not only the season but also the time of the gathering—hence the custom of displaying flowers that are short-lived and indicative of the present moment, which Hounsai so often stresses. Flowers represent a beauty that embraces the moment while accepting and even emphasizing its transitory nature.

Later generations of tea men emulated Rikyu's taste as exemplified in the anecdote about the morning glory tea party. Kobori Enshu is said to have ceased to plant flowers along the roji in order to allow the guests to appreciate the flowers arranged in the tea room.

Morning glories were not the only flowers Rikyu liked to display. The *Nanboroku* tells us something about how Rikyu used flowers: "The flowers of a small room should be one or two of a kind. Of course this also depends on the kind of flowers one decides to display, but the essence is to select flowers that fit into the environment. The same applies to the four-and-one-half-mat room where two kinds of flowers are permissible, depending on the flowers."[2] Rikyu seems to have avoided the Ikenobo-style extravagant display of flowers and preferred a subdued arrangement of one or two flowers depending on the size of the room. Likewise, Rikyu avoided the display of overly fragrant flowers, a rule that the grand tea masters follow to this day. The tradition of prohibiting the use of certain flowers in tea also seems to have begun with Rikyu.

The following verses concern flowers that should not be used in arrangements for tea:

> *Among flowers banned*
> *From the flower vase*
> *Are sweet daphne,*
> *Mountain anise,*
> *And cockscomb.*

> *Patrina,*
> *Pomegranate, waterlily,*
> *Marigold,*
> *And balsam*
> *Are also to be avoided.*[3]

Since the middle ages, Japanese have expressed injunctions like these in the form of easily memorized poetry. About displaying flowers during night gatherings, the *Nanboroku* reports the following: "Since ancient times, people disliked displaying flowers at night tea parties. However, Jo'o and Rikyu discussed the matter and came to the conclusion that, depending on the variety, flowers are acceptable at night meetings as well, as long as they are not colorful flowers, but white ones."[4] Perhaps a white flower, reminiscent of the moon, suits night better than colorful blooms.

Rikyu was, beyond any doubt, an accomplished artist of flower arrangement. One spring, Hideyoshi filled a large bronze vessel with water and placed it in the alcove. Beside it he placed a blossoming branch of plum and ordered Rikyu to arrange the flowers. Hideyoshi's attendants doubted that Rikyu could come up with a convincingly unique and beautiful arrangement, but Rikyu held the branch upside down over the vessel and slid his hand slightly down, knocking off the blossoms. The petals began floating on the surface of the water, creating an elegant sight. Hideyoshi is said to have remarked, "I tried somehow to embarrass that fellow Rikyu, but he wouldn't be flustered!"

Another famous story tells of Sotan and a camellia he had received from a Daitokuji monk. The monk's young disciple was charged with delivering the camellia to Sotan but, unfortunately, the flower dropped off the stem on the way. Having been told to carry the flower carefully, the boy was paralyzed with fear, but finally he decided to deliver both the stem and the flower to Sotan, apologizing for what had happened. When Sotan received it, he placed the stem with a tiny bud still on it in a vase that he hung on the tokonoma pillar. He placed the stemless flower on the floor below it, exactly where it would have fallen naturally. In this way Sotan, known for his intuitive resourcefulness, was able to do the most with the monk's precious gift and the flower's natural lifespan. This episode is a reminder, Hounsai explains, that tea practitioners should not throw away something that is broken or no longer new, but rather should care for all things.

These episodes established a model for subsequent Senke tea-flower arranging. Based on Rikyu's teachings that flowers should be as they are in the field (*hana wa no ni aru yo ni*), Hounsai continues to emphasize that tea flowers should be arranged as if growing naturally in a field. The art of arranging flowers is an art that seeks to reveal eternity by embracing, rather than denying, the thoroughly temporal. "In tea flowers," writes Hounsai, "we attempt to transfer the life of a flower from the field to the tea room. We respect the life of the flower for itself, that life given by nature. When we put the flower into a vase, we try to show it at its very peak of existence."[5]

One must enhance the flower's inherent beauty and spirit. No artifice is warranted. For Hounsai, flowers are "a natural calendar in the tea room."[6] Flowers place the tea gathering in the appropriate seasonal setting by indicating the present season. The host is supposed to go out and gather flowers from their natural environment; hence the expression, "Arrange your tea flowers with your legs." Hounsai reminds us that in the Buddhist spirit of wabi, flowers should also invite the guests to accept the evanescence of all life, including theirs. Like the morning glory, the flower that blooms in the morning but knows of no evening, all things live for a moment. However much they try to outlast time, they cannot; they continue to live in time, ever changing like time itself. All things that try to deny time are fighting a loosing battle against themselves. Hounsai maintains that one cannot go beyond oneself, and this is the ultimate message of tea flowers—if not of tea itself. Tea flowers are like Ii Naosuke's concept of "one time, one meeting," or ichigo ichie. Exactly the same meeting will never repeat itself; the beauty of the moment is what is most important. Yet flowers are not to be understood as mere symbols of our own transient lives; they also carry another, more positive message: they are symbols of eternity that express themselves only within a specific moment of intense life. Through their complete silence, flowers communicate the eternal to us. Nishitani Keiji (1900–90), one of Japan's foremost modern philosophers, has expressed this idea in the following manner: "Finitude itself, in being thoroughly finite, becomes a symbol of eternity. Time itself, in being completely temporal, becomes an eternal moment."[7]

For Hounsai, flowers represent the transience of all life: "So it is with all things, and as a reminder of this, flowers that last a single day are regarded as the most appropriate in the tea room."[8] To realize that all things are short-lived is the very essence of the philosophy of wabi tea. This philosophy helps us become aware that we must do our best to fully realize each precious moment of our lives.

Fourteen Generations
of Grand Tea Masters

Hounsai's ancestors are not merely numbers in a line of blood and artistic descent. They are the building blocks for what tea is today. Without them, Hounsai would not have been able to preserve their tradition, continuing on the path each one of them had prepared for him. In 1981 he acknowledged, "Each of us has a legacy that imbues our lives with meaning in unperceived ways. This gift is the sum total of experiences shared and bequeathed by our ancestors." [1]

SEN RIKYU (1521–91)

Hounsai claims descent from Sen'ami, a doboshu expert in the arts who served the shogun Ashikaga Yoshimasa. The *Senke Yuishogaki*, a family history written by the third-generation descendent of Rikyu, Koshin Sosa, claims Sen'ami to be a descendent of the emperor Seiwa (850–80) and the Minamoto clan. This clan produced the first three shoguns of the Kamakura as well as the shoguns of the Ashikaga period. While the Onin Wars ravaged the capital Kyoto during the years from 1467 to 1477, Sen'ami's family moved to the merchant city of Sakai. There they established themselves as *nayashu*, or warehouse owners, specializing in fish. Rikyu was born in Sakai in 1522. His father Yohei gave him the childhood name of Yoshiro. Later, when he studied Zen under Dairin Soto, head monk of Daitokuji, he changed his name to Soeki. The Buddhist name Rikyu was bestowed on him by the emperor on the occasion of Hideyoshi's tea reception for the emperor in 1585. Soeki studied Ashikaga-style tea under Kitamuki Dochin (1504–62), but later changed to Juko's wabi tea and studied under Takeno Jo'o. Because the records concentrate on Soeki's involvement in tea, one cannot avoid the impression that he neglected his grandfather's fish business and spent most of his time studying tea. Records show that he participated in tea gatherings from the age of sixteen.

He excelled in tea and acquired a reputation in the city of Sakai and beyond. On October 28, 1575 he met Oda Nobunaga for the first time and served him tea at Myokoji in Kyoto. He then became one of Nobunaga's tea advisors together with Imai Sokyu and Tsuda Sogyu, who were both also tea men from Sakai. If it is true that Soeki descended from Sen'ami, one could conclude that he inherited Sen'ami's professional expertise as a doboshu, which his family had maintained for over three generations. Or, it may simply have been Soeki's inherent artistic talents that brought him fame in tea.

After Nobunaga's death in 1582, Soeki became Toyotomi Hideyoshi's official tea master (*sado*). Like Nobunaga, Hideyoshi ruled Japan without relying on official government institutions. Instead, he relied on people such as Soeki to serve as his liaison officers in handling sensitive political matters. On October 7, 1585, in recognition of his receipt of the title of *kanpaku*, Hideyoshi invited emperor Ogimachi to take tea in a tea room that he had had Soeki design and build in the imperial palace. It was on this occasion that the emperor gave Soeki the Buddhist name Rikyu, to allow him access to the imperial palace as a monk. By virtue of assisting Hideyoshi in the imperial palace, Rikyu became the nation's foremost tea master. A few months later, Hideyoshi invited the emperor to tea again; this time, he used a golden tea room he had Rikyu design. In April 1586, Hideyoshi wrote Kyushu daimyo Otomo Sorin a letter introducing Rikyu as his go-between and personal secretary. In the tenth month of the same year, Hideyoshi announced the opening of the Grand Tea Party at Kitano Shrine and heavily relied on Rikyu, Sokyu, and Sogyu to make this large-scale public display of tea and power a success. Rikyu and Hideyoshi's tastes, however, drifted apart from about this time onward.

As the highest-ranking imperial government official, Hideyoshi sought to use tea as a means to display his power and to impress others. As a Zen adept, however, Rikyu strongly inclined towards the egalitarian, simple tea of wabi. A conflict arose between Rikyu and Hideyoshi when the Daitokuji priest Kokei placed a statue of Rikyu on the second story of the temple's main gate (*sanmon*). This was not an unprecedented act; Rikyu had helped finance the construction of the second story, and it was the custom to install statues of the sponsors in the temple buildings they helped build or restore. Hideyoshi, however, complained that he had to pass underneath the temple gate as if trampled by Rikyu's feet. This may have just been a pretext for Hideyoshi to express anger at Rikyu, who opposed both Hideyoshi's taste for lavish tea gatherings as well as his ambitious political plan to attack Korea in order to conquer China. The death of Hideyoshi's brother Hidenaga (1540–91), Rikyu's main supporter, also left Rikyu dangerously exposed to the intrigues of rival factions in Hideyoshi's entourage. As a result, Hideyoshi forced Rikyu to commit suicide. Thus Rikyu died by his own sword on February 28, 1591. The wooden statue of Rikyu is now enshrined at the Rikyu Chapel at Urasenke. The short sword

"Yoshimitsu" that Rikyu used to kill himself in ritual suicide is also in the possession of Urasenke.[2]

From the genealogy of the Furuta family (*Furuta Oribe Keizu*), we learn that, upon Rikyu's death, Hideyoshi ordered Oribe to revise Rikyu's tea, which he felt showed too little respect for the warrior class. After Rikyu had taken his life, Furuta Oribe took over as Hideyoshi's chief tea advisor. Complying with the new social reality and Hideyoshi's political needs, he started what is commonly called daimyo tea.

As official tea master to the two military leaders of the Azuchi-Momoyama period, Rikyu had to serve tea in the formal shoin setting as well as in the more intimate wabi style. Hideyoshi would use both styles, starting with a formal tea in a shoin before enjoying the intimacy of the wabi hut. Though Rikyu may have preferred the wabi style himself, he must have approved of the transition from formal to informal tea. To start a banquet or other public event in a highly formal manner and then relax at the end in an equally highly informal manner has been to this day the norm of Japanese entertainment. In this way, public events end as private ones.

SEN DOAN (1546–1607) AND SHOAN (1546–1614)

After Rikyu's death, the Sen house was confiscated. At that time, punishment automatically extended from the individual to his entire family and family holdings. It was not until 1594 that his family was restored to grace and Rikyu's tea utensils were returned. Rikyu's son Doan inherited the utensils and lived on Rikyu's former estate in Sakai, while Rikyu's adopted son Shoan established himself in Rikyu's former Kyoto residence.

Doan was born to Rikyu's first wife, who died on July 16, 1577. Rikyu remarried the daughter of a Sakai Noh actor whose son, Shoan, had already married Rikyu's daughter and fathered Rikyu's grandson Sotan. Doan made his debut in Sakai as a tea practitioner in 1568, at the age of 23, when Tsuda Sogyu and Yamanoue Soji invited him to tea. Records of a tea meeting of October 15, 1584 at Hideyoshi's tea hut at Osaka Castle show Doan listed among other guests, including Rikyu, Tsuda Sogyu, Imai Sokyu, Yamanoue Soji, and Sumiyoshiya Somu.

After Rikyu's tragic death, Shoan was placed under the custody of Rikyu's daimyo disciple Gamo Ujisato, who together with the future shogun Tokugawa Ieyasu intervened with Hideyoshi to restore Rikyu's family. When this was allowed, Shoan assumed the leadership of the Kyoto Sen family, setting up his headquarters on a lot Rikyu had bought in northern Kyoto, near the temple Honpoji. There he revived Rikyu's hut Fushin'an (present-day Omote Senke headquarters).[3] This resulted in a division of the Sen family into the Sakai and Kyoto branches. The Kyoto branch has flourished until the present day, whereas the Sakai branch disappeared after Doan's death. Doan had only one daughter, who married a merchant. In order to firmly establish the Kyoto school, Shoan retired early in his life in favor of his son Sotan. He drew his main support from the daimyo Hosokawa Sansai and, perhaps even more importantly, from Daitokuji. Shoan died on September 7, 1614. He had one more son, Yamashina Soho (?–1666) who, though a merchant, was a recognized expert on Rikyu's tea utensils.

Genpaku Sotan (1578–1658)

Sotan was born on January 1, 1578 in Sakai. As was customary in Japan at that time, he changed his name frequently—Genshuku, Genpaku, Totsutotsusai, Kan'untei, Fushin'an, and Konnichian—depending on the names of the tea huts or rooms he used or built. Sotan practiced Zen under the monk Shun'oku Soen, the head of Daitokuji's subtemple Sangen'in, and was placed in charge of the temple's store-house.[4] This was two years before the scandal over Rikyu's statue occurred. Rikyu was consulting his friends at Daitokuji as to what action he should take to appease Hideyoshi's anger and, while riding in a palanquin on his way back home, he saw his grandson Sotan cleaning the temple garden. He called him and exchanged some words with him; according to the *Chawa Shigetsu Shu*, this was the last time Sotan saw his grandfather.[5]

Soon after Rikyu's death, the Senke family divided, though the exact year of this division remains obscure. Some scholars believe it was in 1591, the same year Rikyu died; other think 1593 is a more likely date. The only certainty is that as soon as the two Senke families divided, Sotan, determined to continue Rikyu's wabi tea, left the temple and lived with his father at Ogawa, just north of the present Fushin'an. Sotan was barely nineteen when his father entrusted him with the leadership of the new Kyoto Senke family. According to one theory, Shoan retired to a subtemple of Saihoji (now famous for its moss garden), leaving Sotan to live at the Ogawa estate just south of the temple Honpoji together with his grandmother, mother, younger brother, and his two sons, Sosetsu and Soshu. As head of a new tea family, the priest Shun'oku gave him the name Genshuku. When his wife died, Sotan remarried and his eldest son, Soshutsu, left the house, never to forgive his father. His second son Soshu also left the house to become the adopted son of the lacquer merchant Kichimonjiya. Soshu later left his adopted family and founded the Mushanokoji Senke family. Three children were born out of Sotan's second marriage: a girl; then Koshin Sosa, the future founder of the Omote Senke family; and Senso Soshitsu, the later founder of the Urasenke family, of which Hounsai is the present grand master.

Subjecting himself to a strict wabi lifestyle, Sotan came to be known as "Beggar Sotan." He refused honors and, when shoguns and daimyo invited him to teach in their domains, he obstinately stayed on in Kyoto, feigning illness—the only legiti-mate excuse to refuse such an invitation. On the other hand, Sotan tried hard to obtain daimyo positions for his sons. Perhaps this was the only way to secure the future of his family. As a result of Rikyu's suicide, his descendents were insecure and timid for quite some time. Before the consolidation of the Tokugawa power structure in 1615, the political winds could still shift at any moment, especially for those in powerful positions. When Sosa was thirty, he accepted the position of tea master offered to him by the Kii branch of the Tokugawa family. The sixty-five-year-old Sotan accompanied his son to the Kii branch's headquarters in Wakayama. When Sosa was thirty-four and Sotan seventy, Sotan handed the Fushin'an over to Sosa and retired into the backwoods of his estate, building himself a one-and-three-quarter-mat hut he called Konnichian (Today's Hut).

It is said that the name Konnichian came from an exchange of messages between Sotan and Seigan Soi, the one-hundred-seventieth abbot of Daitokuji. Sotan had invited Seigan to visit the new hut, but he was late and arrived when Sotan had already left. Therefore, Seigan left a note that said, "I am a lazy monk, but I came to see you today rather than tomorrow. I regret to have missed you." To this Sotan replied, "Since you came, I wish I could have met you today rather than tomorrow." He selected the "today" out of this exchange to name his newly built hut.

Sotan also sent his younger child Soshitsu into daimyo service. The Maeda family of Kaga Province (present-day Ishikawa Prefecture) sought his services as an expert in tea utensils. Sotan added a four-and-one-half-mat tea hut called Yuin and the eight-mat Kan'untei for Soshitsu. The Urasenke ("Rear Sen Family") lineage developed out of the support these buildings provided. Fushin'an became the headquarters of Omote ("Front") Senke and Kankyuan, built along Mushanokoji street, of the Mushanokoji Senke schools.[6]

Sotan's retirement to the Konnichian was, for him, a return to the practice of Zen he had experienced as a young man at Daitokuji. The following poem expresses the kind of Zen tea Sotan had adopted:

> *Tea appeals to the heart,*
> *To the eyes and to the ears,*
> *And not a single word needs to be written.*[7]

Thus, Sotan mused on the Zen reluctance to rely too much on language.

Sotan once painted Daruma (the Indian monk Bodhidharma), revered as the founder of Zen. This painting is still in the Urasenke collection. Sotan did not make an elaborate painting, but just a sketch, a drawing, perhaps taking only a few seconds, of the contours of Daruma's body, accompanied by calligraphy. This painting represents the Zen-inspired simplicity and wabi that Sotan was seeking in his life. The wabi lifestyle he pursued became the basis of Urasenke and a number of other tea schools.

Sotan died on December 19, 1658 at the age of eighty-one after having composed this death poem:

I was born out of emptiness
As an empty fellow,
And now as the temple bell rings,
I return to emptiness.

SENSO SOSHITSU (1622–97)

Senso Soshitsu was Sotan's last son. Sotan was forty-five when he was born. Senso (all subsequent heads of Urasenke bore the name Soshitsu) first studied Chinese medicine under Noma Gentaku and called himself Genshitsu, taking the "Gen" from Gentaku. When Gentaku died unexpectedly, however, Genshitsu returned home to his father Sotan and trained in Rikyu's tea. Then, at the age of thirty, he received the name Soshitsu. Before Sotan died, he bequeathed to his son the Konnichian, Yuin, and Kan'untei complex that now constitutes the Urasenke head-quarters. Senso inherited the wabi life and tea style from his aged father Sotan. Thus, Senso became the heir of Rikyu's wabi tea and one of Rikyu's foremost legitimate descendents. He accepted a position that the daimyo of Kaga Province (present-day Ishikawa Prefecture) had offered him, but he rarely left Kyoto and continued his father's lifestyle. After he had celebrated the thirteenth funeral anniversary of his wife and father (both died in 1658), the new Kaga daimyo, Maeda Toshitsune, offered Senso a new position as *chado bugyo* (tea commissioner). Toshitsune was a cultured man who had already studied tea under the Confucian scholar Kinoshita Junan (1621–98). Senso went to Kanazawa accompanied by a Raku potter. In Kanazawa, Senso remarried and, at the age of fifty-two, fathered a boy who was destined to become Joso Soshitsu, Rikyu's fifth descendent and head of Urasenke. The year before his elder brother Sosa and his half-brother Soshu died, Senso had to shoulder the responsibility of continuing the Sen schools. He was therefore unable to stay in Kanazawa permanently and went back and forth between Kyoto and the daimyo's castle town, making the journey one hundred and forty-two times between 1681 and 1688. In 1687, he submitted his resignation and was able to settle permanently in Kyoto at the age of sixty-seven. Even after he had entrusted Urasenke affairs to his son Joso, he returned to Kanazawa several more times.

Senso was known for the utensils such as tea bowls, tables, and kettles that he designed, inspired by the objects he saw during his frequent trips to Kanazawa and back. In 1690, he built a chapel for Rikyu in his compound to celebrate the one-hundredth anniversary of Rikyu's death. This memorial service helped establish him as the legitimate heir to Rikyu's tea and promote Rikyu as the father of all tea. On January 23, 1697, while in Kanazawa, Senso felt he was nearing death and composed the poem:

> *As an empty fellow,*
> *I came riding on emptiness,*
> *I now return*
> *At the sound of*
> *The early morning bell*

He was seventy-six.

JOSO FUKYUSAI (1673–1704)

Rikyu's fifth descendent in the Urasenke line was Joso Fukyusai. He was born in Kanazawa, married at the age of twenty-one, and had a boy, the future Taiso Rikkansai. When Senso died in Kanazawa, Fukyusai was twenty-five.[8] The Kaga authorities asked him to continue in his father's footsteps and he became the second chado bugyo to the daimyo. Yet when he received an offer from the Hisamatsu daimyo family of Iyo Province (on the island of Shikoku), he accepted and became the first to serve the Hisamatsu family in a line that continued until the Meiji Restoration of 1868. The daimyo of Kaga thought that Shikoku might offer the sickly Fukyusai a better climate than the bitterly cold Japan Sea coast and suggested the transfer. The two hundred and fifty bushels of rice he received from the Hisamatsu in addition to his income from the Maeda family came to a considerable amount, especially given that he stayed in Kyoto most of the time and often fulfilled his duties in absentia. Whenever he did go to Shikoku, Fukyusai indeed had better health despite his busy schedule. He also had to work hard for the upkeep of the Urasenke school in Kyoto.

Fukyusai lived during the Genroku era, which is considered a period of the renaissance of many Japanese arts. His designs of new utensils, such as tea containers and candle holders and trays, were often painted in vermilion. Like his father, he commissioned the Raku kiln to produce tea bowls and water containers to his taste and design. He was also an accomplished calligrapher. His life was too short to develop his taste to the degree that it could make a lasting impact. He died on May 14, 1704 at thirty-two.

TAISO RIKKANSAI (1694–1726)

Rikkansai was the sixth-generation descendent of Rikyu. When his father died, he was merely eleven years old. Genso Kakukakusai of Omote Senke, who was twenty-seven then, prepared Rikkansai for his future leadership by accompanying Rikkansai in numerous tea gatherings. When Genso conducted the twenty-fifth anniversary of Sosa's death at Omote Senke's Zangetsutei tea room, there was a memorial tea contest during which Genso was host and the twenty-two-year-old Rikkansai was the main guest. Though eleven years younger, Genso's eldest son Joshinsai and Rikkansai became good friends. Knowing that Joshinsai liked moxa treatment, Rikkansai had a craftsman make a tray of the dry, kneaded grass that is used in moxa, and presented it to his friend at a tea meeting at Konnichian. Rikkansai studied the Chinese classics under Ito Togai (1670–1736), a celebrated expert in Chinese poetry and an amateur performer of Noh and Kyogen; he also made his own tea bowls and was a talented calligrapher. He served the Hisamatsu daimyo of Matsuyama. Rikkansai lost his wife when he was only thirty-two, just before he traveled to Edo to take up residence at the Matsuyama clan's Edo headquarters. Edo's humid climate and Rikkansai's busy schedule took their toll on his health. He died in Edo at the age of thirty-three and was buried at Tokaiji temple in Shinagawa.

Chikuso Saisaisai (1709–33)

Saisaisai was another short-lived head of Urasenke. While Rikkansai was still in Edo, his mother and younger sister waited for his return to Kyoto, hoping to arrange a marriage between Rikkansai's sister and Genso's second son. The news of Rikkansai's death in Edo prompted the sister to take vows and to retire to a Buddhist nunnery called Saihoji, a temple whose famous well Rikyu had used during Hideyoshi's Grand Tea Party at Kitano Shrine. Her Buddhist name was Sosen. She later became the temple's abbess and continued to pray for her brother's afterlife.

Rikkansai's mother was left alone at Urasenke and adopted Genso's second son Saisaisai from the neighboring Omote Senke family. As new head of Urasenke, Saisaisai could rely on the assistance of his father for only a short time, as Genso died only four years later, when Saisaisai was twenty-two.

Saisaisai is known for adding a five-mat room called Mushikiken (No Color Room) to Konnichian. He displayed a work of calligraphy in the room that read, "The colors of the pine, now and then unchanged." He died aged twenty-five on March 2, 1733, and his adoptive mother died the following year.

Itto Yugensai (1719–71)

Yugensai was also adopted from Omote Senke. He had been Genso's third son and Saisaisai's younger brother. He did much to enhance the cause of the Senke schools with the help of his Omote Senke brother, Joshinsai. He was fifteen when his brother Saisaisai died, so Joshinsai helped Yugensai to develop his talents, especially in his early years. They both practiced Zen meditation at Daitokuji and, as the iemoto system developed, they devised the so-called Seven Ceremonies.

Yugensai had a far greater impact on Urasenke than his two short-lived predecessors. He repaired Konnichian and invited Daitokuji monks to a tea party there. Yugensai's wife died at twenty-five and, in 1746, his second wife bore him a son. Yugensai enjoyed studying the Chinese classics and the Noh theater.

Joshinsai, the head of Omote Senke, died in 1751, when Yugensai was thirty-three and his heir was only eight years old. Therefore, when it came time to celebrate the one-hundredth anniversary of Sotan's death, Yugensai assumed the leadership over all the Senke schools.

As leader of the Senke schools, Yugensai attracted many disciples. By this time, the Hisamatsu daimyo had become an important patron of Urasenke. Yugensai also acquired disciples from the Hachisuka daimyo family of Awa Province (now Tokushima Prefecture on the island of Shikoku) and attracted interest among officials of the Edo shogunal government and among Edo merchant families. He sent his top disciples to serve in other parts of Japan. One of them, Hayami Sotatsu, whom Yugensai sent to serve the Ikeda daimyo family as tea master, wrote many tea books at a time when publications on tea were popular. Yugensai's disciples helped establish the Senke schools in many parts of Japan. Yugensai died on February 2, 1771 at the age of 53.

SEKIO FUKENSAI (1746–1801)

Fukensai was twenty-six when his father Yugensai died. On January 1, 1788, when Fukensai was forty-one, a fire broke out near the Kamo River at Shijo and burned for three days and three nights, reducing nine-tenths of Kyoto to ashes. People at Urasenke had enough time to take their belongings to safety before the fire reached the compound. Fukensai and his family escaped unscarred to Daitokuji. The foremost duty of the Senke iemoto was to rebuild the buildings and tea rooms. On August 22, 1788, repairs began to restore Yuin and other buildings at Urasenke, enabling the iemoto to organize a number of commemorative teas for the bicentennial anniversary of the death of Rikyu, which took place between September 22, 1789 and March of the following year. Fukensai invited the iemoto of Omote Senke and Mushanokoji Senke, including nobles, daimyos, priests, and other tea people. Fukensai rebuilt Urasenke exactly as it was before the conflagration. The statue of Rikyu had been flung into the pond in front of the chapel to save it from the flames, and it had to be repaired when it was recovered from the pond. When the repairs were finished, an "eye-opening" ceremony was held to reconsecrate the statue, providing the occasion for a large tea party. Fukensai died on September 26, 1801 at the age of fifty-six, leaving three children. Among them, his eldest son inherited the position of Urasenke iemoto, and his third son, Kokosai, became the sixth iemoto of the Mushanokoji Senke school.

Hakuso Nintokusai (1770–1826)

Nintokusai married a girl of a well-established family of Kibune in the northern mountains of Kyoto. She bore Nintokusai a son when he was seventeen. Marrying young and producing children as soon as possible after the marriage was necessary in an age when the average life span for a man was less than forty years. Begetting an heir early in life was one assurance of the transmission of know-how and tradition from father to son. When Nintokusai was twenty-five, old enough to receive the secret teachings from his father, he broke with precedent and wrote all these teachings down. Fukensai scolded his son, reminding him of Sotan's poem that one should learn tea with the body and not through any writing. Nintokusai then burned all his notes. Nintokusai became the Urasenke iemoto at the age of thirty-five. After his father died, it was he who had to transmit Fukensai's teachings to Fukensai's younger children. When Nintokusai's son was seventeen, he entered Daitokuji to practice Zen but, in 1811, he died before his parents. Nintokusai had five more children, all of whom died. He therefore decided to adopt a son of the Matsudaira daimyo family of Mikawa Province (present-day Aichi Prefecture), who was to become Seichu Gengensai, one of the greatest Urasenke iemoto. As a rule, any Sen family without a suitable heir adopted a son from another Sen family. But at this time the Sen had no available male offspring, and so a son of a daimyo family was adopted.

Nintokusai died on August 24, 1826 at fifty-seven, and his wife on July 8, 1844 at the age of sixty-seven.

Seichu Gengensai (1810–77)

Nintokusai was already fifty when he adopted Gengensai, the son of a daimyo, by marrying him to his daughter in 1819. Nintokusai wanted his adopted son to study the Chinese classics, the Kongo school of Noh drama, calligraphy, incense, and poetry, in order to give the future iemoto a broad education that would benefit Urasenke tea, but Nintokusai died when Gengensai was only fifteen. Nevertheless, Gengensai took over Urasenke leadership with vigor. One of the important events in his early career was the two-hundred-fiftieth anniversary of Rikyu's death, to which he invited many people, including a prince, several nobles, and monks. Memorial tea services were established by Sotan as a means to establish iemoto authority on a broad basis. In preparation for this event, Gengensai undertook several building projects at Urasenke. He built the gate, the tea rooms Totsutotsusai, the six-mat Daironoma, the twelve-mat Hosensai, and the Baishian tea hut. Rikyu's memorial services involved all Senke schools but, since Gengensai was the eldest of the three iemoto, the responsibility fell on his shoulders. As a member of the samurai class, Gengensai continued his services as tea master to the Maeda and

Hisamatsu families. In addition, he received a stipend from the Kii branch of the Tokugawa family and transmitted the secret teachings on how to use the daisu table to the head of the Kii branch. Gengensai also served as tea commissioner of the Owari clan of the Tokugawa family.

In 1844, Gengensai lost his stepmother. The following year his first wife died, but her younger sister, who had become his second wife, bore him a son. This son died at the age of seventeen. Left without an heir, Gengensai adopted a son of the Suminokura family, a wealthy Kyoto merchant family, by marrying him to his daughter. This adopted son became the twelfth-generation Urasenke iemoto Yumyosai.

Gengensai lived during a difficult period in the history of tea. Tea had already declined at the end of the Tokugawa period despite sporadic efforts to revive it. In order to understand the transition of tea from the Tokugawa to the Meiji period (1868–1912), we must briefly discuss the political history of the period. Only then can we appreciate Gengensai's tea.

The Meiji Restoration of 1868 brought an end to the traditional shogunal government, which had ruled Japan since 1185. The old imperial government, first established around 645 and strongly modeled on Chinese government, was restored. Japan's centuries-old reliance on Chinese civilization, however, gave way to influences from the West. In order to defend herself against encroaching colonial powers such as England, France, Germany, and Russia, Japan industrialized quickly. All this brought about a change in values and, in many cases, a destructive negligence of Japan's traditions. As tea had been heavily patronized by the warrior class, it declined when that class was officially abolished.

In the early Meiji period, tea came to be looked upon as a frivolous pastime. In 1872, Kyoto Prefecture levied a tax on local trade and granted licenses to increase regulation. At this time grand tea masters were licensed as "genteel entertainers" (*yugei*). Confucian thought looked down on entertainment as low and unworthy of a gentleman, and officials of the new government classed tea as entertainment. Gengensai protested against this categorization. He submitted a manifesto entitled *Chado no Gen'i* (The Original Intent of the Way of Tea), expounding the highest ideals of tea. He defended tea as a Way useful for character formation and ultimately for the state. However, no tea master has ever served as member of the official Academy of the Arts (Nihon Geijutsuin). After the Meiji Restoration, the Sen schools lost their daimyo support and had to fend for themselves.[9]

As the traditional schools declined in the early Meiji period, *sencha* (steeped tea), the favorite tea of the Edo-period intellectuals, became increasingly popular. In November 1875, for example, Kumagai Suikoo, a wealthy incense manufacturer, convened a sencha gathering in Kyoto's Maruyama district at which 478 art objects and scrolls from 132 families were put on display. Several thousand people are said to have drunk tea at the twenty-four parlors. Sencha attracted people by emphasizing large-scale tea gatherings rather than imitating the small ones of the Senke schools. The three Sen schools also participated in some of these large-scale gatherings—for example, in the one organized at the imperial palace beginning on March 15, 1876, which lasted one hundred days.

As the government shifted its attention toward the West, Gengensai looked desperately for ways to save tea. For the International Exhibition of 1872 in Kyoto and its foreign visitors, Gengensai devised a tea in which both host and guests sat on chairs. This marked the birth of the so-called ryurei method of preparing tea on a table. By 1875 Omote Senke had followed suit. Gengensai also devised several portable tea-box sets, contributing to the popularity of tea in the new age. Gengensai also opened tea to women. Since women were excluded from public functions under the previous warrior government, they had not been allowed to participate in formal tea meetings.

Hounsai wrote in 1983, "Gengensai was a person able to look ahead. He lived in a difficult time of political transition. He had the vision to adapt tea to the modern age."[10]

Several years ago, the city of Okazaki, where Gengensai was born, unveiled a statue to commemorate his services to tea. Since Gengensai enjoyed a relatively long life, he not only trained his adopted son but also his grandson in the Urasenke traditions of tea. This ensured the continuity of Urasenke tea in the new age.

Jikiso Yumyosai (1852–1917)

Like his predecessor Gengensai, Yumyosai lived in a difficult time for such traditional arts as tea. During this period the new government propagated a nationalism based on Shinto, and one way of revitalizing tea was to offer tea to Shinto shrines (kencha). The custom of offering tea at Shinto shrines began in the late 1880s with offerings to Kitano Shrine, perhaps in commemoration of Toyotomi Hideyoshi's Grand Tea Party of October 1, 1578, at Kitano Shrine. Senke grand tea masters also began offering tea to Buddhist temples (kucha), for example at Kozanji temple on the six-hundred-fiftieth anniversary of the monk Myoe's death. Despite these efforts, tea continued to decline.

Yumyosai, a son from the Suminokura family, was twenty when Gengensai adopted him. After training in tea, he taught tea to old aristocratic families and in women's schools, helping to popularize tea among women. In 1885 he retired, handing over Urasenke affairs to his eldest son. Until his death in 1917, he lived at various places, among them the temple Myokian. Rikyu's famous Taian (Waiting [for Hideyoshi] Hut), built in the years 1582 and 1583 originally at Yamazaki Castle, was now attached to Myokian. Yumyosai also lived at Daitokuji. Yumyosai's life spanned a difficult period. The Suminokura family declined rapidly in the new age and he was forced to sell Urasenke treasures to make a living.

Tetchu Ennosai (1872–1924)

After Yumyosai retired early, it fell on Ennosai to further tea in Japan's modern age. Hit by hard times, Ennosai moved to Tokyo and, as recorded by his second son Iguchi Kaisen, lived without even sufficient rice and salt—the minimum staples of traditional Japanese life. The eighth-generation Mushanokoji grand tea master Isshisai Soshu (1848–98) and twelfth-generation Omote Senke grand tea master Sosa Rokurokusai (1837–1910) also lived in poverty, selling precious tea utensils from their collections to eke out a living. As if this were not enough, a new school of tea arose and split away from the Sen families through the efforts of Tanaka Sensho (1875–1960), who established the Dai Nihon Chado Gakkai (Japan Association of Tea Ceremony). Tanaka Sensho studied under Ennosai, but at the age of twenty-three he left the school, criticizing the iemoto system as based on secret teachings, and set himself up independently. Such an action would have been inconceivable during the Tokugawa period, with its highly stratified feudal system, but was now possible in a new era of radical political and social change. Sensho also advocated a return to the spiritual values of tea, and he reevaluated the role of tea in society, using Confucianism and Zen Buddhist teachings. He tried to circumvent the classification of tea as a "genteel entertainment" by developing a tea devoid of the framework of feudal society. He also made effective use of the new mass media to make his school known throughout Tokyo.

Yet, despite many handicaps and hardships, tea began to flourish again and found sponsors among a class of nouveau riche businessmen. The new patrons of tea were the wealthy merchants who followed the example of Matsudaira Fumai in collecting famous utensils. Among them were Masuda Don'o of Mitsui and the politician Inoue Kaoru (tea name: Segai, 1835–1915). The latter contributed effectively to the revival of traditional culture by inviting the emperor and empress to his home and entertaining them with Kabuki and tea in the new tea hut he had constructed for the occasion. The precedent for this was Toyotomi Hideyoshi's invitation of Emperor Ogimachi to his newly constructed golden tea room. Inoue's tea party marks the entry of tea into the high society of the new era. The new political leaders were again using tea as a vehicle to promote smooth human and political relations. By 1900, tea had been recognized as one of the great traditional arts of Japan. In that year a group of wealthy merchants and politicians created tea associations in Tokyo and Osaka. Interestingly, none of these gatherings included the traditional iemoto families.

Surprisingly, it was women who returned prosperity to the iemoto system. In 1907, Gakushuin University, the university of the patrician class, included tea instruction using tables and chairs, tea procedures in Japanese-style rooms, flower arrangement, and tea preparation in its female student curriculum. Tea also became a part of the regular curriculum at girls' schools in Kyoto. Between 1920 and 1930, the tea-practicing population grew increasingly female. In 1936, Yukosai Soshu, the tenth-generation Mushanokoji Senke grand tea master, spoke on tea for the first time on the radio. The accompanying textbook sold 175,000 copies.

At the beginning of the twentieth century tea also formed part of the Japanese drive to create a national identity. It had defeated China in the Sino-Japanese War (1894–95) and was about to challenge the Russian positions and ambitions in East Asia. After it had assimilated Western technology, Japan was able to look inward to discover its own traditions. For Masuda Don'o it was particularly painful to see with what speed and quantity Japanese art was being exported. He wrote in his *Jijo Masuda Takashi Den*: "The reason why I collect art objects is of course because I like it, but also because, in order to develop Japanese art, it is necessary to carefully keep samples in Japan and to study them. That is why I feel I need to buy as much as I can. If not, foreigners will take away all of it and nothing will be left in Japan."[11]

It was in this age that Ennosai became an important leader in the world of tea. Ennosai was only thirteen when Yumyosai retired. At eighteen he married a girl of the noble Kuki family. Convinced that the future of tea was in Tokyo, he shuttled between the two cities and his first son was born not in Kyoto but in Tokyo. It was under his leadership that the first monthly tea journal appeared, the *Konnichian Geppo*. Like his father, he tried to include tea in the curricula of girls' schools. He had started to offer an intensive summer-school course in tea at Urasenke, and it was during the thirteenth session that he collapsed and died. He was fifty-three.

SEKISO TANTANSAI (1893–1964)

Tantansai was Ennosai's eldest son and heir apparent. Under his leadership, tea came to be firmly established in the new age. Like his predecessors, Ennosai had to practice Zen at Daitokuji as soon as he came of age. The monk in charge gave him the Buddhist name Mugensai, but he later changed it to Tantansai, a name given to him by the noble Kuki family. He had the opportunity to serve tea to the empress at Daitokuji and to the crown prince at one of Katsura Imperial Villa's teahouses. This was the beginning of a close link between Urasenke and princes Takamatsu, Chichibu, and Mikasa.

Tantansai continued serving offertory tea to temples and shrines throughout Japan, beginning with the imperial ancestral shrine at Ise. In so doing, he was updating an ancient syncretic Shinto-Buddhist practice that may go back as far as the monk Eison, a contemporary of Eisai who, in 1239, offered tea to his temple's protective Shinto deity, Hachiman. This was rather unusual, given that saké had been the customary offering to Shinto deities. He also extended the practice of holding memorial tea services to include people other than Rikyu. In October 8, 1936, the Showa Kitano Ochanoyu was held at the three-hundred-fiftieth anniversary of Hideyoshi's Grand Kitano Tea Party. About one hundred tea parlors were built. On April 21, 1940 the Sen families held a large-scale Rikyu anniversary gathering at Daitokuji. More than five thousand people came to the three-day event highlighted by a memorial tea at Daitokuji's Lecture Hall (Kodo). The iemoto used such grand tea gatherings to enhance their authority.

Tantansai continued his predecessors' efforts to propagate tea in private schools and Hounsai has continued this work. Tantansai, Hounsai's father, was the first tea master to try to propagate tea abroad. He "dreamed of visiting China" (Hounsai's words), the birthplace of tea, but the political situation prevented him from carrying out his plan. He did travel to the United States and Europe, giving lectures and demonstrations, though he never changed his kimono for Western dress. Shortly after the war, in 1947, Tantansai established the International Chado Cultural Foundation as a commitment to making tea international. He also taught A. L. Sadler, an Australian, who later wrote *Cha-no-Yu*, perhaps the first comprehensive book on tea in the English language.

Tantansai worked to solidify tea in Japan, and in 1940 he founded the Tankokai association and branches, organizing Urasenke tea people in various parts of Japan. He was known for his impeccable taste and had his ten craftsmen (Senke Jusshoku) make many tea utensils on the basis of his designs.[12] He designed three tea huts and built large *dojo* (halls of practice) in Kyoto and in Tokyo. In 1946, just after the war, he made Urasenke into a legal foundation (*zaidan hojin*) called Konnichian. One of its purposes was to preserve Rikyu's heritage. In 1957 he was decorated by the emperor, the first such honor ever bestowed upon a tea master.

In 1980, Tantansai's wife died after a long and debilitating illness. Her name was Kayoko and she was given the posthumous Buddhist name Seikoin. She was perhaps the first iemoto wife who took an active part in Urasenke's daily activities, assisting her husband whenever she could. She received her education in Sendai and brought a modern Western self-esteem and a strong will to Urasenke. Her presence did much to establish the wife of the iemoto as an important position. Tea was still a traditional and male-centered world; she entered it in a delicate manner, never embarrassing her husband or tarnishing his public image. She pushed for the promotion of the first female *gyotei* (highest-ranking disciple of the iemoto), Hamamoto Soshun (d. 1986), who became one of the most revered tea teachers at Urasenke and personal tea advisor to present grand master Hounsai. Through the Soroptimist International movement, of which she was a cofounder, she tried hard to improve the position of women in Japan. She, too, was honored by the emperor in recognition for her contributions to the understanding of traditional arts in modern Japan.

In spite of an attempt by the Allied Headquarters to close the Tankokai, the association of prominent Urasenke supporters, World War II did much less damage to tea than did the Meiji Restoration, and tea flourished together with Japan's postwar economic recovery.

Hounsai can look back upon a rich history of tea to which he is directly related. He is called upon to live this heritage and to transmit it to future generations.

part two

Hounsai: The Life of a Grand Tea Master

The Life of Hounsai

CHILDHOOD

Grand Tea Master Hounsai was born April 19, 1923 into a family that had dedicated itself to tea for the preceding fourteen generations. Masaoki (his childhood name) was the third child born to Tantansai and his mother, Ito Kayoko, who was from a samurai family that had served the daimyo of Sendai. As the first two children had been girls, the then current grand master Ennosai was happy to have a male grandchild to carry on the family tradition and he celebrated this auspicious event with a tea meeting at Kyoto's Heian Shrine. Ennosai died the following year, succeeded a year later by his wife, Hounsai's grandmother Tsunako, the daughter of a daimyo family. Masaoki's "Sendai Grandmother" was a disciplinarian. She had received tea instruction from Ennosai and had trained her daughter-in-law (Masaoki's mother) in the strictest fashion.

In the Sen-family tradition, the future heir had special status and was raised separately from his brothers and sisters. Kayoko did not like this old custom and, after consultation with Tantansai, decided that Masaoki should grow up with his brothers and sisters so that, in the future, they would be able to rely on a strong bond among themselves. Masaoki was therefore brought up together with his siblings in a large, happy family. Due to Ennosai's untimely death, Tantansai became iemoto at the age of thirty-one. He had the reputation of being an extremely honest and sincere person, to the point that he was said to be overly rigid. Hounsai said of his father, "He led a model life as the head of a tea house, and pursued this single calling throughout his life." [1]

As future heir, Masaoki underwent various ceremonies from his early childhood. The first was the *hakamagi*, "the first donning of *hakama* trousers." The ceremony, held when Masaoki turned five, required the child to prostrate himself on the floor, wearing the unaccustomed long, trailing hakama trousers and, trying not to trip on

them, asking each guest for their kind favor. It must have been painful and stress-
ful for the young boy to maintain a proper posture throughout the ceremony, but
this was training for his future life as a tea master.

From early childhood, Masaoki was surrounded by tea. He played in tea rooms
and even in the forbidden tokonoma alcove. As a child he was naturally curious
about his environment and tested everything; his parents thought him mischievous.
We can imagine him sticking his finger into the carefully prepared ashes in the bra-
ziers, or even through the paper windows—something almost all small children do
in Japan. But most important, from the very start he grew up in the environment
of tea.

In accord with Urasenke tradition, Masaoki received his first tea lesson at the age
of six, on the sixth day of the sixth month. As he had not yet entered elementary
school, these lessons were the first rigorous routine Masaoki had to undergo. Without
his father's permission, he had already learned how to fold the fukusa, a silk cloth
used for cleansing the tea caddy and the tea scoop. His father taught him to prepare
and serve tea by holding Masaoki's hands in his and putting him through the movements again and again. After just one lesson, Masaoki was forced to serve tea in front
of guests, who encouraged him by saying, "*Omedeto gozaimasu!*" (congratulations).
From that day on, Masaoki was permitted to receive tea lessons and, on occasion, to
attend his father when he had guests and to carry the tea bowls to them.

Masaoki's first lessons were about the handling of tea utensils, something especially hard for children to learn. He comments, "I remember the time it took my
teachers to get me to hold my pen in the right position or my mother to teach me
how to bind my shoelaces." Beginning regular lessons so early is indispensable for
the proper functioning of the iemoto system. To learn tea under the best available
teachers and from an early age allows the future iemoto to have a technical and
perhaps even aesthetic edge over all others and to exercise authority in tea. His
sheer skill gave him the much-needed authority to preserve a traditional ritual art.

It is easy to imagine how hard it must have been for Masaoki to learn some of
the more complicated tea procedures at this early age, but the earlier the training
begins, the more thoroughly tea procedures become part of oneself. Only by adapting one's body and mind to tea can one grow into tea and acquire the authority of
a grand master. Tantansai preferred to teach his son with hands-on practice rather
than verbal instruction so that the procedures would become a part of him and
would not be quickly forgotten. During Masaoki's first lessons, his teachers allowed
him to handle tea utensils freely, so that he could develop a feeling for their proportions and learn to care for them in a proper manner. By learning how to handle
tea utensils, Masaoki learned how to respect them. His parents taught him that
utensils are not toys but important family treasures to be used again and again by
future generations of grand masters.

He had to learn how to bow. In tea there are three types of bows, the formal, semi-formal, and informal bows. In the formal bow, the entire palm touches the floor and the body leans proportionately forward; in the semi-formal one, only the fingers; and in the informal bow, used among guests, friends, and old acquaintances, only the tip of the fingers. Masaoki's parents only gradually taught their young son the more complicated procedures; they tried to avoid alarming him with the apprehension every child feels when first confronting obligations and tasks.

Masaoki was literally raised in the tea room. Like his predecessors, Masaoki had to practice tea while other young children spent their time playing. No doubt, he envied the other children and hated the strict discipline his father imposed on him at such an early age. Masaoki wished for an escape and, after entering elementary school in 1930, he started lessons in other arts, such as *komai*, a short dance of the traditional Kyogen theater, and calligraphy. One day, Yoshiharu, Masaoki's younger brother, wanted to go to the calligraphy lesson too but, having nothing to do while his brother was writing, jiggled Masaoki's arm and disrupted the lesson. Masaoki took his brush and smeared some ink on Yoshiharu's face. The teacher was mad and scolded Masaoki that calligraphy brushes are not to be used to smear ink on people's faces and was about to send him home for good. Masaoki had to apologize profusely to be readmitted to his calligraphy lessons.

Children cannot be expected to take things too seriously; their world is play. One day, Masaoki brought home some of his elementary school friends and took them into the Urasenke tea rooms to play. His mother admonished him, saying, "Don't step on the tatami mats!" "Why not?" asked Masaoki. His mother explained to him that they were mats used only for the preparation of tea or for guests. Tatami borders represent boundaries, she said, and respect for boundaries is the wellspring of courtesy and deference. But Masaoki was still too young to understand this reasoning.

Masaoki and his brother Yoshiharu liked to play Tarzan by tying a rope to a branch of the pine tree in the garden and swinging from it. Once, the bark of the tree got torn away and the culprits were discovered in no time. Their mother grabbed them by their collars, pulled them down the hallway, and finally threw them into the storehouse in the back. When things got out of hand, she would bundle up their bedding and have them carry it on their backs, declaring, "I'm sending you to Daitokuji for good, right now!" Yoshiharu would inevitably cry in despair, "No, no!" Daitokuji was the site of the Sen-family temple and Rikyu's grave, and Yoshiharu was particularly afraid of the temple. Knowing that one day he would have to undergo rigorous Zen training at Daitokuji, Masaoki was less frightened; after all, one day he would have to go there anyway. Like most older brothers, Masaoki strongly disliked being scolded for his brother's misadventures.

When Masaoki was nine, his Sendai grandmother came to stay at the house to improve her mastery of tea. One evening after supper she was practicing koicha (thick tea). Half out of curiosity, Masaoki peeped into the room, whereupon his grandmother had him enter and sit down, and proceeded to let him drink a bowl of thick tea. Hounsai recalls that when he went to bed that night, "my head was buzzing, probably from the tea, and a strange thought entered my mind: People are living because they are breathing, but what exactly am I, this person who is breathing here? Of course, I could not come to an answer, and I was overcome by fright."

The next morning, Masaoki asked his mother, "What does my existence as a human being mean?" This profound question from such a young boy took her by surprise, and she asked him why he came to ask himself such a question. When Masaoki explained the circumstances to her she told him to try praying for an answer to his question. She told him to always be grateful for the good fortune to live and enjoy another day of life. From that time on, even during school outings, Masaoki prayed regularly, in times of happiness and hardship alike.

In most modern Japanese families, it is the mother who is in charge of educating her children, and children spend most of their time with their mothers. The fathers are busy working, often until after the children are asleep, and except on Sundays, many fathers see their children rarely. Masaoki's situation, however, was different. His father took over his tea education from an early age, and no one, not even his mother, was allowed into the room while he taught Masaoki. But Kayoko felt she had a stake in her son's upbringing and tea training, so she often listened outside the door to her son's lessons. She did this so that she could repeat the instruction later or make it somewhat more understandable to the boy. She had more patience than her husband and would not give up until her son had grasped all his father had tried to impart to him. Hounsai recalls that his mother knew just by listening whether he was walking correctly, with a sufficiently distinguished manner suitable to a future grand master, during his lessons. With her sharp powers of observation, keen interest, and tremendous patience, Kayoko played an important auxiliary role in Masaoki's tea education.

In order to master the art of walking in a tea room, Masaoki practiced carrying a small ceramic brazier filled with ash in an upright position as he walked. This practice allowed Masaoki to walk with the correct demeanor, not too lightly but with balance, grace, and respect for the tea environment. Learning how to walk properly in the tea room is an important part of tea training; walking as one would on the street is impermissible, and noisily sliding over the mats, producing a swishing noise, is equally inappropriate. Walking in the tea room must be elegant and apparently effortless.

Tantansai rarely played with his son. Occasionally when they passed each other in a hallway he patted his son's head and asked if everything was going well. At times when Tantansai was tired of appraising tea utensils and writing certificates in his best calligraphy, he would go into the garden to relax. For Masaoki this was the opportunity to entice his father into some kind of play and, for a short while, they might play catch or another such game. Playing with his son brought relaxation and a happy smile to Tantansai. But these were rare occasions, and generally Tantansai had little time for his son outside of lessons. The ever-growing population of tea practitioners kept him busy and completely involved with his official duties. Masaoki remembers his father as a rather stern man who, when busy, would push him away, even when he was seeking help with homework. Yet this was also part of Masaoki's education, teaching him the need to be independent and self-sufficient in all things. *Amae* is a Japanese term used by some Japanese psychologists to explain a tendency to rely heavily on others; it is a trait that even adult Japanese display. Tantansai knew the danger of amae, and he made a conscious effort to prevent his son from developing it. Given his responsibilities, a grand master must be a fiercely independent leader.

Twenty-three years after the death of Tantansai, Hounsai recalled an incident that vividly illuminates his as a father.

> I recall one cold winter night when my brother and I, still children, were in the bathtub, and we heard the sounds of wood being fed into the outdoor furnace for heating the bath. Taking for granted that it was the household helper, I called out that the bathwater was hot enough. A voice came back, "All right, all right"—my father's voice! Opening the window, I saw my father out there in the cold night, wearing just a thin nightgown, feeding firewood into the bath furnace for us. Humbled, I told him please not to bother; I would look after the bathwater. However, his reply was, "No, no, that won't do. Heating the bathwater is the same as heating water for tea; if the person heating it changes, the regulation of the temperature will change, too." And then he resumed his position stooping in front of the furnace. [2]

This was how his father applied the rules of tea to his everyday life.

EDUCATION

When in 1936 Masaoki entered Doshisha Junior High School, jealous fellow students often remarked, "Hey Sen! You're lucky, you know? You won't have to choose a career. It's all decided for you already. You don't have to study to get into a good university like the rest of us. And even if you decide to go to a university, it doesn't really matter which one, does it?" Masaoki wished they knew how utterly unlucky he felt, and he brought a friend home with him and revealed everything about the position to which he was destined to succeed. There were so many events Masaoki had to attend at Urasenke, including the Summer Training Session. Realizing the difficult duties that lay ahead of him, his friends gradually teased him less and even came to sympathize with him. Toward the end of junior high school, when his friends were deciding what they wanted to become—doctors, army officers, and so forth—Masaoki was rather envious of what he conceived of as the privilege of choosing one's own career.

Although the Sen family was affiliated with the Zen sect, Masaoki's father and then Masaoki attended the Christian Doshisha Junior High School. Doshisha was founded by the celebrated Japanese Christian leader Niijima Jo (1843–90), whose wife had studied tea under Ennosai. Niijima and his wife were therefore frequent visitors at Urasenke. At Doshisha there were obligatory chapel services, sermons, religious study classes, and classroom prayers, including mandatory Saturday Bible Study. It was at this school that Masaoki was initiated into Christianity, which helped him to understand people of other nations and cultures. Among his teachers was Takahashi Tsutomu, a former naval captain and a devout Christian. His wife was a friend of Masaoki's mother, so the families socialized with each other. Takahashi was the teacher of Masaoki's worst subject, mathematics. Takahashi therefore invited Masaoki to his home to help him catch up and, sometimes, to a dinner of sukiyaki. Takahashi tried to instill in his pupil an interest in mathematics and reprimanded him for not trying harder to study even those subjects he disliked. Thanks to Takahashi's patience and perseverance, Masaoki improved in mathematics and geometry.

In junior high school Hounsai took up riding. Tantansai enjoyed riding and he thought that his son should adopt a sport to strengthen his body. His father had let him ride from time to time, even as a child. As soon as he entered junior high school, Masaoki joined a riding club to improve his posture and control. "It was difficult to control a horse on the riding field or at the hurdles with only reins and inner resolve, but the joy of acquiring the skill gave me a feeling of grandness beyond description," Hounsai wrote, reminiscing about his youth. Riding also involved free movement in open space, whereas tea had to be practiced sitting in a closed, confined environment. Riding also helped him develop mental and physical balance. In his last year of junior high school he inherited a horse called Chihaya. "Riding around on Chihaya was the joy of my life," he recalls. However, many of the club's horses, including Chihaya, were drafted for army service and Masaoki was forced to help the army to train horses. Many of these horses came from the countryside; some were unruly and would bite, kick, and rear up, giving their trainers a hard time. If a trainer happened to let go of a horse's rein, the supervisor would beat him with a bamboo stick as punishment. If he mounted wearing spurs, the supervisor would shout: "Horses are military equipment. How dare you possibly injure one!" Masaoki later learned that Chihaya fell ill and died during military service. After the war, Masaoki obtained another horse and competed in the National Athletic Meet on two occasions. Hounsai presently serves as President of the Kyoto Equestrian Federation and as Vice-President of the Japan Equestrian Federation.

Another sport Masaoki immersed himself in was judo. He reached the fifth-level rank in the upper division. He writes that he switched to judo from fencing because he "did not like getting hit on the head." Sports were an escape from tea and a way to prove himself to his colleagues as more than just the pampered heir of a famous family. Although he preferred school over tea during junior high school, Masaoki learned how to live in two radically different worlds: academics and athletics at school and tea at home. All of this hardened and strengthened his body and his mind.

Another important ceremony awaited the sixteen-year-old Masaoki: *genpuku*, or initiation into adulthood. In premodern Japan, boys had their forelocks shaved for the first time and received a new name at this ceremony. According to Urasenke tradition, however, initiation involved offering tea to the gods (kencha). On December 1, 1938, Masaoki presented a daisu temae at Kitano Shrine, preparing tea at a small table, coached by his father:

> A frigid winter wind was blowing through the shrine; I felt tense at having a public audience, and my body trembled. Once I began the temae, however, those things disappeared from my thoughts, and I remember that all I was conscious of was the pounding of my heart. I only prayed fervently that I would be able to prepare tea well, and, somehow managed to make good of the training that, in preparation for this day, I had received over the previous year.

As he grew older, Masaoki had to attend more Urasenke events, and often he had to sit for hours, just watching. For this, he blamed Rikyu, who is supposed to have said "Learn the Way of Tea by watching!" Iemoto in many traditional Japanese arts instruct by having their pupils imitate the master, and Masaoki felt he was a victim of this practice, too. Later, however, as grand master, he too came to affirm the importance of this principle. One cannot learn tea with the mind and memory alone; one must learn it with one's body. A tea person must become one with tea.

Hounsai recalls an incident that illustrates this point admirably. He had already begun taking lessons from one of the senior gyotei tea teachers, but he felt that his father, as the most accomplished tea master, should teach him, not an ordinary assistant. He went to Tantansai to ask him why he didn't spend more of his time teaching him. Tantansai said nothing, but the look on his face indicated his deep displeasure. He took Masaoki to the small dark room where a statue of Rikyu was enshrined and made him sit before the altar and pay respect to his ancestor. He then scolded his son:

> Just because you were born to this house does not mean that you will become its master effortlessly. You must, from the start, be strict and severe

in developing the Way for yourself. To that end, although the man who stands before you is your father, in these things I am not your father but the grand tea master, practicing and training in the Way of Tea. To tell it to you simply, as long as you pursue this path, I am your teacher. You are taking advantage of the fact that I am your father and you ask me why I do not give you instruction. If you truly want to learn, come and ask me properly like a student requesting instruction from a teacher.

This was the beginning of a new relationship between Masaoki and his father: that of master and disciple. From then on, whenever his father was available, Masaoki asked him for instruction in the formal master-disciple manner, by bowing so deeply that his forehead touched the tatami. This was to initiate Masaoki into not just tea procedures and the proper handling of utensils, but the true spirit of tea.

In order to teach his son the need to respect all things, even inanimate ones, Tantansai told his son the following story.

When I was eight, I and my father and grandfather, the fourteenth, thirteenth, and twelfth grand masters respectively, went to a shrine in Tokyo to offer tea to the deity. My father promised me that if I performed the offertory tea ritual without making mistakes, I could have anything I wanted. As an eight-year-old boy, I had been longing for a brass bugle and, with the intent of making it mine, performed a flawless ceremony. My joy upon receiving the bugle was boundless and I took to blowing it with all my might. Perhaps I had only meant to rinse out the mouthpiece when I found out that I could also use the bugle to shoot out water. After a while this little game ruined the bugle. "You performed the ceremony very well and as a result received a brass bugle. No matter how happy you were, it is a wretched thing to break it." In fear perhaps that I might do the same to precious tea utensils, father reprimanded me. "If you truly aspire to the Way of Tea, it is a serious error to break things or treat them carelessly." I could not even utter an "Erh" to this, and from then on I actively requested to receive lessons. My father was an extremely strict teacher when it came to tea lessons. Though he might say, "This is plenty for now," he would demand that I go through the lesson again, and make me continue until it seemed as though my legs were no longer my own.

Masaoki's lessons were equally severe. On cold winter days, he had to practice proper tea walking by walking barefoot along the tatami-floored hallway leading to Rikyu's chapel. The feet have to slide lightly over the mats. "The cracks I got on my feet then have become hard lumps now," he recalls.

Five years into junior high school, Masaoki wanted to go to university in Tokyo, away from home, tea, and Kyoto. His mother would not allow it, and so Masaoki decided to take the entrance exams to Waseda and Gakushuin University, both located in Tokyo, in secret. He managed to get permission from his mother to go to Tokyo with a friend. They stayed at the home of his uncle, who was a rear admiral. He asked Masaoki why he and his friend had come to Tokyo, and Masoki had to reveal the truth. When the rear admiral heard what was going on, he scolded Masaoki: "I understand how you feel, but this is not the proper way to do things. Without your parents' approval I cannot let you stay here." Masaoki managed to take the exams anyway, but under pressure from his parents he had to give up his plans to study in Tokyo. And so, in the spring of 1941, Masaoki entered Doshisha University in his hometown of Kyoto. His parents wanted him to study history or archeology, but he preferred economics. This time his parents had to give in. He also took German, which seemed to him more masculine than French. As a university student, Masaoki turned into a voracious bookworm. He enjoyed reading poetry and avidly read Hermann Hesse and Shimazaki Toson. He would often go book hunting whenever he had some spare money, or he borrowed books from his friends.

Masaoki's junior high school years coincided with the era when Japan was beginning to tread the path of militarism. The liberalism of the Taisho (1912–26) and the early Showa (beginning in 1926) periods was coming to an end. Just prior to Masaoki's enrollment, the February 26 Incident (*Niniroku Jiken*) took place, and in July of the following year (1937), the Sino-Japanese War broke out, sparked by the Marco Polo Bridge Incident (*Rokokyo Jiken*). Because Doshisha was a Christian school, the military kept it under close scrutiny and the commissioned officers assigned to the school increased the severity of the military drills to which all male students were subjected. Dr. Yuasa Hachiro, who in 1935 joined the school as chancellor, was forced to resign after only two years. He had received his education in the United States and was a known liberalist, opposing military fascism.

THE WAR

Just as Masaoki was matriculating into college, the Pacific War broke out. It was still a while before Masaoki reached conscription age, so he spent his free time listening to music in coffee shops or watching movies. There was a crackdown on minors smoking and food was getting scarcer. At the school cafeteria, the choices on the menu were dwindling and the only dish available was often *kitsune donburi*—thin slices of deep-fried tofu over rice. Sometimes there was curry rice, or rice with a cutlet of some dubious kind of meat on it. Masaoki sometimes invited hungry friends to his home, where his mother would cook them sukiyaki, regarded at that time as a special delicacy. Several of his friends enlisted in the training corps.

When they came back on home leave in their noncommissioned officer's uniforms, they looked quite impressive, and Masaoki increasingly felt the call to serve his country. He eventually enlisted as a trainee hydroplane flier.

In April of 1943, the hydroplane training center at Zeze near Lake Biwa in Shiga Prefecture was commissioned by the Japanese military to recruit the first group of pilot trainees from universities. Masaoki attentively read the announcement on the school's bulletin board. The offer had its attractions: trainees were exempt from school military drills and training started at 1:00 PM, lunch provided. Telling his mother that the application was for glider training, he got her to sign the parental consent. After interviewing Masaoki, the officer in charge, Lieutenant Kageyama, told him that he thought he was fit and patted him on the shoulder, saying, "Work hard!" Masaoki's friends also passed, and from the next day the commute to Zeze began. Their training consisted of an hour of basic lectures on aircraft and related subjects, followed by cutter training, naval gymnastics, and flag signaling. After two weeks, Masaoki experienced his first flight. He had to dress in the proper pilot's attire: a flight suit, a parachute belt over a life jacket, short boots, and a flight hat. "Looking at my reflection in the large mirror that was there for us to check on our posture," he recalls, "I felt I was actually a pilot now. . . and, if I dare say so myself, I was quite pleased with what I saw."

When it came to flying for the first time, Masaoki was so nervous that his instructor noticed it. "Don't be so nervous!" he said to comfort him. "There is hardly any chance that we'll crash. If there is an emergency, let me handle it!" Masaoki calmed down and was able to fly comfortably. But his instructor was watching him keenly. "The instant I seemed to feel a bit buoyant," he writes, "I was whacked with a bamboo sword from behind."

Masaoki learned how to control the aircraft. The instructor told him to move the control stick as if it were part of his body. Handling an aircraft was, as Masaoki found out, like handling tea utensils: it must be as automatic as if the controls were extensions of one's body. Then on September 20, Aviation Day, Prince Kayanomiya came to inspect the training center and Masaoki flew his plane solo in view of the prince. The newspapers reported the story, and Masaoki's mother finally knew that her son was not flying gliders as he had pretended, but the more dangerous hydroplanes. He got a good scolding from her when he came home. "That was unmanly of you!" she said, angered at least as much by the deception as the danger.

Training turned out to be so hard, made even harder through the competition among trainees from different universities, that Masaoki felt that "marching with a rifle at the school drills would have been easier." Soon after the Student Mobilization Act was made public, students were no longer exempt from conscription and Masaoki had to take the physical examination for conscription. In December he was drafted into the navy, and his college life came to an abrupt end after only two years. On December 10, 1943, Masaoki enlisted in the naval corps and was sent to the naval base at Maizuru.

> Upon entering the corps, I was at once disappointed by the uniform I received. For second-class sailors and below, like me, it was a common sailor suit without even a rank badge; the type of uniform they called *jonbera* (jumper) or *karasu* (crow). I had imagined that I would immediately be allowed to wear one of those sharp-looking officer's uniforms with a short sword hanging at the side, but that expectation proved to be too hasty.

It was corps policy to group members according to the schools they had attended, hence the fierce rivalry that developed among the units. Training was extremely hard, and there were tests day after day. To make things worse, students of literature and law had to take tests in mathematics and physics, subjects that they did not specialize in. Thanks to his good eyesight and his training as a hydroplane pilot, Masaoki passed the exams and, on January 25, 1944, was assigned to Tsuchiura Naval Air Corps as a reserve student of the Fourteenth Special Flight Unit.

Masaoki was then able to wear the officer's uniform that he had so yearned for, although it came with many hardships and further aptitude tests. After Masaoki completed officer's training, he had to undergo a strange test: a thorough analysis of his facial features. The examining officer simply stared at Masaoki's face as he was told to turn to this side and then that side. After the test, Masaoki was sent to reconnaissance. He could not understand how someone who got an A in the hydroplane test could be assigned to reconnaissance. Upon inquiry he was told that the signs on his face revealed impending death and that a large percentage of similar cases had died of accidents. There was nothing Masaoki could do but follow the "Three S's" of the officer's code of conduct: be smart, steady, and silent. He accepted his assignment with grace but lingering regret.

In May 1944, two hundred trainees including Masaoki were transferred to the naval air force base in Tokushima Prefecture and began training as reconnaissance officers. After duty, Masaoki and other trainees would often take the bus to go to the city of Tokushima, where they enjoyed good food. Pay in the navy was good and chief pay officer Utsumi Hitoshi took good care of the trainees; later, unfortunately, he was transferred to aircraft-carrier duty. (After the war, Utsumi had a remarkable career and worked himself up to the position of Director of the National Personnel Authority.) One of Masaoki's duties was to board reconnaissance planes and assist the pilots in navigating the planes to their destinations and back. He recalls his responsibilities at that time, saying, "Skill in navigation is crucial in getting a plane safely to its destination. The slightest error could have serious consequences. We made our calculations checking the cruising speed, direction of the wind at each altitude, the coordinates of our destinations, and so forth. We had to do this assidu-ously, and so it was quite a job."

Masaoki also had to practice shooting at drogues drawn by planes, and he liked this mock fighting best of all. As the war was drawing toward its end, Masaoki's training intensified, including night flights and dive bombings. The unit was assigned to Okinawa and, by the spring of 1945, it seemed to Masaoki that he would soon have to engage in real fighting. To overcome their sense of imminent danger, Masaoki and some of his colleagues would go out at night, face home, and call out "Mother!" in a loud voice. "I will never forget how," he wrote years later, "through the expression in our eyes when we looked at one another, we communicated and shared our emotions." Hounsai bonded powerfully with his fellow officers, and he never forgot them. In 1979 he established a club for the surviving members of the Fourteenth Special Flight Unit and they have tea once every two months at the Urasenke Tokyo Center.

On April 2, 1945, the first group of men from the Tokushima Naval Air Corps Special Attack Unit were ordered to fight at the front, but Masaoki's name was not on the list. Nishimura Ko, later a popular actor, reminded Masaoki of their pledge to die together, and Masaoki tried to get enlisted too, but he was instead transferred to a division in Matsuyama. There, as an assistant divisional officer, Masaoki had to instruct seventeen- and eighteen-year-old trainees. Some of them went to the front as Special Attack Force (suicide) fliers, never to return. Others, though they were pilots, were assigned as marine Special Attack Force personnel, and manned human torpedoes.

Masaoki was not unmoved by their plight, and he wrote, "Although I never knew when they would order me to the front, it was heart-wrenching to sit in a circle with them and make tea, and then send them off." After the war, the celebrated writer Mishima Yukio once asked Grand Master Hounsai whether he could prepare tea on the battlefield.[3] He seems to have been unaware both that Rikyu had to serve tea to Hideyoshi and his generals over the smell of gunpowder and how many times Masaoki served tea to his colleagues about to fly into death.

In May, the Matsuyama base was bombed, and Masaoki had to live for a while in a local elementary school. It was here that he received his standby order. However, the opportunity to fight at the front or to dive his plane into an American warship never came, and by August 15, 1945, Japan surrendered.

On May 1, 1946, in Tokyo, Masaoki saw Nishimura Ko walking in the May Day Parade, representing the actors union. "I heard a voice call out, 'Sen!'," he recalls. "Looking around to see who could possibly be calling out my name at a place like this, I saw Nishimura waving his hand. . . . I barged into the line, we hugged, and I continued walking in the parade with Nishimura as far as Shinbashi." As he found out later, Nishimura actually set out on his Special Attack mission but made a forced landing and was able to return safely. The others in his circle who cried out

"Mother!" all died in action. "Today, I still remember the faces of my comrades-in-arms who executed their suicide missions out there over some part of the Pacific Ocean. I wish to keep that experience of my youth nobly stored within my heart. . . . This is what I honestly feel."

Masaoki was in Matsuyama when the news of the end of the war reached him. He left to report to the army administrative office near Himeji and there he was simply told: "Go home!" And so he did. In October 1945, after serving for two years, Masaoki reached his home at Ogawa Street in Kyoto. Upon seeing him, his mother nearly fell to her knees. His parents had not known his whereabouts and were uncertain whether he was dead or alive. His younger brother Yoshiharu, who had been discharged earlier, thought that his older brother had died in the war when he smelled incense on entering the house, and that he must now take over his brother's duties. He was therefore overjoyed to see his older brother alive and well.

Masaoki and Yoshiharu's first task at Urasenke was to tear down the bomb shelter that had been built in the garden. This was a way for Masaoki to overcome the despondency he felt after coming home from the war.

> Something that both startled and irritated me once I got home after the war was the presence of the Occupation Forces. Probably they wanted to see something authentically Japanese and approached our house as though they were visiting a museum. They drove up to Konnichian in jeeps and asked for tea to be prepared for them to drink. Since I had been a part of the Special Attack Unit, the intrusion of these men into our house was unbearably discomforting. I even disdained to see their faces.

Tantansai would not refuse anyone who came to visit and he calmly hosted these men. With the English he had learned at Doshisha, he explained how to behave at a tea meeting, how to bow to the host if you are a guest. Then he had them sit properly on the tatami. They all obediently followed Tantansai's instructions. Among these Americans were some rude young men who lay down on the mats, even using the alcove board as a pillow, but once reproved by Tantansai they followed his instructions precisely. At the end of tea, Tantansai would order them to leave. Impressed by his dignified bearing, the soldiers would leave respectfully. Japan may have been occupied by the Allies, but at Urasenke, Tantansai was the unquestioned boss. Seeing this, Masaoki was impressed by his father's strength and determined to pursue the way to seek understanding and peace. "Having survived the war, this was my mission," he told himself. At this point, his discomfort with American soldiers waned. "I realized how foolish it was to bear hatred toward people." This realization marked a turning point in Masaoki's thinking after the war that was to color the rest of his life and career.

The war had interrupted Masaoki's education for two years. He returned to the Protestant Doshisha University in Kyoto and finished the remaining year in economics at the Department of Law. At first it was hard to resume studies as if nothing had happened. The school was full of veterans, mostly still in uniforms. They would prefer talking about their war experience, rather than spend their time studying. They talked about their dead comrades, or about those who were taken prisoners by the Soviets. Many students were poor and those close to graduation had neither work nor prospects. This was not the time to set one's eyes on employment in a large and secure company. Masaoki did what he could to find employment for his friends.

Masaoki graduated in September 1946 and found a job as a teacher in a girls' high school for a monthly salary of fifteen yen. As a naval officer, his salary had been close to two hundred yen, including peril compensation. This salary was less than ten percent of his former salary. Fifteen yen was enough to buy three loafs of bread. After ten months on his job, Masaoki lost his position as a result of the Allied Occupation Headquarters policy on education: the headquarters wanted to discourage schools from hiring former army officers. Masaoki therefore moved to Tokyo, where he studied tea art as a special staff member of the Nagao Museum. This museum was founded by the former president of Wakamoto Pharmaceutical Company, Nagao Kin'ya, who had collected important tea utensils. Masaoki was allowed to live at Nagao's residence. He recalls this time in his life: "Every morning I would pick up a few flowers from the many that bloomed in the big garden and place them in the tea room, hang up a scroll, and prepare the utensils for tea."

Masaoki was free to use any utensils but, from time to time, Nagao would instruct him about utensil combinations. He often served tea to Mr. and Mrs. Nagao and their guests. In those days, the Nagao Museum was offering art consultation, and many Americans came to have them evaluate their purchases of Buddhist statuary, paintings, and calligraphy or antique objects of all kinds they purchased in the countryside. Masaoki, too, served part time in that office. It was here that Masaoki got much-needed training in art appreciation and learned how to distinguish authentic works from fakes.

ZEN TRAINING

Masaoki was now twenty-five and it was time for him to undergo Zen training and to become a Zen monk. This was a prerequisite for assuming the role of Urasenke grand master. Since Rikyu's time it was customary for tea masters to be trained in Zen in order to be able to assume the spiritual leadership in the Way of Tea. Goto Zuigan Roshi, an old acquaintance of Masaoki's mother, had just retired from his position as head priest of Daitokuji and lived a secluded life at Jukoin, a subtemple of Daitokuji. Rikyu's ashes had been interred at Jukoin. Its Kan'inseki, a tea room allegedly designed by Rikyu, stood for its commitment to tea. "I was grateful to be able to study with such a noble, well-educated priest and outstanding man of Zen," Hounsai wrote later in his autobiography. The roshi told him that despite his experiences as a soldier he must become again like a naked child or no effective training could take place.

This was also the occasion for Masaoki to give up his childhood name and assume a tea name in order to become wakasosho, or future grand master. Goto Roshi gave him the name Hounsai Genshu Soko Koji. "Hounsai" means Phoenix Cloud; the legendary phoenix was believed to be a protector of Buddhism. He also had to undergo a traditional ceremony in which he reported to his ancestor, Sen Rikyu, his resolve to become the next grand master. On that occasion, his father gave him the box of transmission but warned him not to open it before becoming the actual head of Urasenke. Later, when he became grand master, he found in the box a list of all fourteen generations of grand masters in their own handwriting. When one writes one's own name on this list, it is believed, one receives the spirit of the ancestors. As wakasosho, Hounsai assumed a more important role in Urasenke. He was now allowed to sit three meters away from his father during tea gatherings at the Totsutotsusai tea room; prior to this, he was not even allowed to enter it.

In reference to his new position, Goto Roshi gave Hounsai two instructions: "Become like the inkstone that does not wear away no matter how many times one rubs it," and "Demand! And then avidly seek to know!" In addition to these religious instructions, Goto Roshi told Hounsai never to act as if he knew everything about tea.

Hounsai also received two important *koans* (a word, phrase, or story upon which monks concentrate to try to break out of conventional thinking and find enlightenment) from Goto Roshi. The first had a message designed specifically for Hounsai. After he became a Zen monk, Hounsai began his lifework: the internationalization of tea. In 1951, Hounsai traveled to the United States for the first time. Ever since he attended junior high school, he had dreamed of learning foreign languages and spreading the Way of Tea abroad. When he informed Goto Roshi of his plans, the roshi gave him the koan, *"Shujinko"* (Master). This was a koan based on a story about the Chinese monk Ruigan (pronounced in Japanese as Zuigan) whose name Goto Zuigan Roshi had adopted. The koan takes the form of a monologue by Ruigan:

"Master," he called to himself.
"Yes, yes," he answered.
"Master! Be warned against the deceptions of others around you. Aren't you doing something that will cause them to talk behind your back?"

And then he abruptly said, "Master. Were you dozing just now?"

"No, I was not," was his reply.

This koan is a reminder that we must be our own masters, and in giving Hounsai this koan, Goto Roshi wanted to remind him to discover himself, especially now that he was able to look at himself and at tea from abroad. Hounsai still displays the calligraphy of this koan at important tea meetings, such as Rikyu's memorial services.

The second koan, called *Zanmai*," emphasized the importance of singular concentration on one's path toward enlightenment. It was given to him by Goto Roshi's successor Kajiura Itsugai of Myoshinji temple.

TRAVEL ABROAD

Inspired by the transmission of tea from China to Japan, Hounsai dreamed of transmitting it to the American public. The times had changed and, as he wrote, "it was no longer a time you could enclose yourself in a tea room." Hounsai especially wanted to contact those Americans who had visited Urasenke before the war and had studied under his father and grandfather. Among them were the Scottsfields, who in 1905 had their daughters Helen, Grace, and Florence undergo tea training at Urasenke. They later built a teahouse in the United States, though the location is unknown. Also Tantansai had donated some teahuts to American Buddhist churches and other community centers before the war, but in general only Japanese Americans had access to them. Few Americans not of Japanese descent had ever heard of tea. With the support of his father and his Zen teacher, he determined to go.

Endorsed by tea devotee Brigadier General Dike of the Occupation Forces of Japan, Hounsai was given the necessary travel documents (at that time Japanese had no passports) from General Douglas MacArthur's headquarters in Tokyo to travel abroad. Tantansai had made up a list of Americans with an interest in tea and gave it to his son with enough money to enable him to live in the United States on three dollars a day. Hounsai recalls his preparations for the trip:

> Like a young schoolboy sent on an important errand, I placed my precious
> list carefully in a large bag that I would never be parted from. In the bag,
> my mother also tucked in a small charm bag that she had sewn and, as a
> final safeguard against any unlikely event, a small diamond she had kept
> hidden away.

Except prominent Japanese such as Suzuki Daisetsu (Daisetz), the Nobel Prize winner Yukawa Hideki, the industrialist Matsushita Konosuke (an Urasenke sponsor), and his own university teacher, the Christian educator Yuasa Hachiro, there were few Japanese allowed to leave the country under the Allied Occupation, which lasted from 1945 to 1952. As a citizen of a defeated nation, Hounsai did not expect to be welcomed and planned to provide for his basic, everyday needs himself. He brought a portable tatami mat on which to serve tea; he also carried a message of peace, a scroll with the characters for "Harmony, Respect, Purity, and Tranquility" that his father had written. Before his departure, Hounsai prayed at Urasenke's Rikyu Chapel for a safe journey, hoping that Rikyu would inspire him to do the right things abroad. Hounsai went to the United States to show the true democratic heart of tea to Americans, who continued to think of Japanese as barbarians.

Hounsai left Japan on October 10, 1951 and arrived safely in Hawaii. His daily allowance was far too little to get by; fortunately he found many tea people who invited him to stay at their homes. Hounsai quickly realized what many travelers had realized before him—that travel to foreign lands and exposing oneself to unfamiliar languages and customs is a way to discover oneself. He understood that different people attach different values to things: "What the Japanese think of as strange, is not at all strange here and things that are so natural to the Japanese that they are not even conscious of it, are looked upon as strange over here." Later Hounsai also came to see teaching tea to Americans as a way to polish his own tea.

The reports Hounsai sent home from the United Sates were published in the monthly tea journal *Tanko*. Reading these reports, one gets the impression that Hounsai sought to fulfill two roles while in the United States. One was to inform the Japanese tea people of his activities, the interest in tea he encountered among Americans; the other was to inform Japanese readers about the United States in general. After the war, the United States had become Japan's model for democratic change and industrialization. The image of the United States Hounsai provided was a positive one: "America is an experimental nation, a nation of progress beyond the mere distinction of the complete and incomplete."

Being in the United States allowed Hounsai to compare East and West and, in this process, he became a cultural go-between. He felt that being in America helped him to fully realize the strengths but also the weaknesses of his own nation and of traditional Japanese culture. He was particularly drawn to the American concept of personal privacy (which he summed up as the philosophy of "Mind your own business!") and the clear demarcation between the private and public worlds that comes with it. For him, this demarcation was far too blurred in Japanese culture. "If one does not understand this, one cannot enjoy life in the United States," he wrote.

He also realized that for civilization to move ahead men must understand and work together with women. Japanese tea, he thought, had become too much of a men's world. At the same time, his upbringing in the world of Japanese tea had instilled in him a sense of human equality and egalitarianism which, as he wrote in his reports home, astounded the somewhat old-fashioned Japanese-Americans he happened to meet in Hawaii. In one of his reports he approvingly quotes his friend, the sculptor Isamu Noguchi: "What the Japanese need most of all to learn from the Americans is to try to understand things from a wide perspective." Hounsai wrote that although he understood the meaning of what Noguchi told him, he realized it more and more as he went along. He also felt that Americans make a greater effort to understand other cultures and that Japan was still lacking a true concern for the world at large. Later, visiting the Library of Congress in Washington, Hounsai discovered, for himself and for his Japanese readers, the history of the United States. He noted in particular a happy coexistence of the individual and society that he found lacking in Japan.

Another role Hounsai adopted while in the United States was to reflect on Japanese traditional culture from an American perspective. Americans were eager to learn about something as exotic as Japanese tea, whereas his countrymen were only too willing to give it up. Hounsai warned his fellow Japanese not to sacrifice traditional culture for what he called an ill-understood, superficial Americanism.

After two months in Hawaii, Hounsai left on March 17 for the mainland United States. The DC 4 flight was still long and tedious. In Los Angeles, as in Hawaii, Japanese Americans who had practiced tea before the outbreak of the war offered him a warm welcome. What impressed him then would no longer impress any Japanese visitor: the city's flashing neon signs.

Hounsai's trip to the United States was not just tourism. He met with the mayors of several major cities and delivered letters from the mayor of Kyoto—always in his Japanese formal dress of *haori* and and hakama (a kind of overcoat and trousers).

Whereas some Hawaiian Japanese had Japanese tatami rooms in their otherwise Western-style homes, on the mainland he often had to serve tea in improvised settings. Placing a straw mat over a carpet was the only way to create something even approaching a proper atmosphere for tea. Hounsai took this challenge as a positive stimulus. He felt that teaching tea in an environment lacking in the basic elements of traditional tea permitted him to improvise in the way Rikyu had always urged: "If there is no lid rest, look for something like it in the kitchen, be it only a salt or pepper shaker."

The lack of beautiful dishes for serving kaiseki food proved to be a serious problem for Hounsai. Following Rikyu, the food had to be simple, but he wanted to make up for the plainness of the food with beautiful dishes and food display, as was customary in kaiseki. Unless this was possible, he felt, the host could not communicate with his guests through the medium of artistic appreciation—which is, of course, the essence of tea. In one of the more successful tea meetings in Hawaii, he served the following kaiseki:

> Entrée: Hawaiian clam with a salad of raw fish and cucumbers and
>   chopped ginger.

Soup: Miso with small Hawaiian yams with black sesame
Rice: White Smith rice
Boiled food: Egg tofu, shrimp, and green beans
Fried food: Minced beef eggroll (Hawaiian style)
Soup: Plum with water shield

He served these dishes not on the usual *hassun* (square tray), but on the kind of square trays commonly available in the United States. In Japan, the chopsticks used in tea had to be made of green bamboo. This was not available in Hawaii, so Hounsai had to use a similar local product. The setting for the meeting was as follows:

Calligraphy: *"Hibi Kore Kojitsu"* (Day by Day, Every Day Is a Good
    Day), by Tantansai
Flower vase: Hibiscus in a yellow Seto-ware vase
Kettle: "Tsurukubi" (Crane Neck) Kettle. Name: "Tetsuyatsure" (Worn-
    out look)
Water container: Bizen
Tea container: Old container with Kodaiji-type lacquer design
Tea scoop: Made by Tantansai. Name: "Mushin" (No Mind)
Bowl: Black Raku made by Keinyu in a Hagi kiln
Cake: Aloha dumpling

In this way, Hounsai combined Japanese and Hawaiian styles, adapting tea to the environment in which it was being served. In so doing, he felt he was following Rikyu, who advocated the adaptation of tea to the immediate circumstances rather than imposing a rigid norm. Rikyu expressed these thoughts in the following poem:

Tea is nothing but
Boiling water
And making tea.
This is the only rule
You should know.[4]

Fourth-generation Urasenke iemoto Senso added to this, saying "by breaking the rules, one realizes for the first time the importance of the rules." Based on such principles, Hounsai made it his task to propagate tea abroad, despite the often completely different physical and cultural milieus. Hounsai comments on this challenge: "Tea is made for the Japanese house, with its feeling of purity and calm, but because the American house differs so much, I must find a way to do tea in an American house. The best method of achieving this is the *ryakubon*." "Ryakubon" is serving tea on a tray; it could be done without the design and accoutrements of a Japanese room.

Though Hounsai's English steadily improved, it was often insufficient to explain tea philosophy to the American public. He seems to have become effective at communicating nonverbally, however, and he reports happily that one day, after a lecture in Los Angeles, a girl approached him saying that she understood what he wanted to say by watching his gestures, facial expression, and attitude. But he was well aware of his linguistic shortcomings, and reports with humorous chagrin that he sometimes failed to understand what it said on the menu in restaurants and he took chances and ended up receiving something he did not like or want.

While in the United States, Hounsai realized that tea had a universal appeal and could adapt to any culture; he also concluded that anyone could become a genuine tea practitioner regardless of gender, nationality, culture, or religion. Later, in 1958, he wrote home about the various types of foreign tea people he encountered: "Among them you find the Belgian who inquires about Japanese etiquette, the American who says that he had been invited many times to tea in Tokyo, the German who combines tea and the Way of Warriors (Bushido), the British gentleman who is well versed in tea and manners, and the talkative Frenchman who enjoys the quiet atmosphere of tea." He was convinced that tea could bring out the best of any culture or personality, and he strongly argued against the preconception that only Japanese were able to understand and appreciate tea. "In the Way of Tea, . . . there is no difference between whether one is Japanese or not; the only difference that exists in tea is whether one is a *chajin* [tea practitioner] or not. I know from experience that this is true."

For Hounsai, tea calls out to be internationalized precisely because people of all nations can understand and appreciate it as well as any Japanese. Later, Hounsai wrote that "there are a number of non-Japanese who are true People of Tea, having eagerly and conscientiously undergone training in the strict rules of etiquette, and having grasped the inner spirit of the practice."[5] At times Hounsai even seemed to credit non-Japanese with perhaps more facility in tea than they deserved, as happens when Japanese tell foreigners just starting to learn the Japanese language that they speak better than natives: "Compared to the depth of understanding shown by people of other countries, however, I am not so sure about the level of understanding that today's Japanese possess regarding the spirit of tea."

One of Hounsai's goals in transmitting tea to the United States was to enrich American lives with the spiritual and aesthetic communication offered by tea, contributing a quiet, contemplative serenity to the hurried daily pursuits of materialistic society. While in the United States, he established new Urasenke branches and revived prewar ones. In March 1951, the Hawaii, Los Angeles, San Francisco, and New York chapters held their first postwar tea gatherings. This was followed by similar ceremonies in Brazil, Argentina, and Mexico in 1954. In April he traveled to Seattle to lecture and offer tea at a Japanese exhibition at the Hut of the Murmuring Pine, which he had donated for the 1962 Seattle World Exhibition. At the same time, he organized the Seattle chapter and offered its members both day and night classes.

On May 8, Hounsai offered tea at the Women's Faculty Club of Columbia University in New York. Dr. Yukawa Hideki, at that time Japan's only Nobel Prize laureate, introduced Hounsai and other Japanese Americans who were among the guests. This was followed by a demonstration in Lakewood, New Jersey, at Georgian Court College, which had a Japanese garden and a tea hut in a state of severe disrepair. Hounsai directed the repairs needed to be able to use it for tea. On the May 19, Hounsai offered a memorial tea for the war dead at a Buddhist temple in New York.

The highlight of Hounsai's 1953 visit to the United States was his tea service to the foreign and Japanese delegates who had gathered to sign the San Francisco peace treaty in March of that year. Hounsai was delighted by the news that his native Japan was finally going to be again an independent nation, and he was convinced that the idea of tea for peace had borne fruit. He wanted the world to know that in tea Japan had a tradition of both democracy and peace. This gave Hounsai the opportunity to carry out, through Rikyu's tea, a kind of cultural mission. At a time when Japan's foreign diplomacy was still very timid and largely undefined, Hounsai saw the need for Japan to pursue a cultural diplomacy, and he firmly believed that tea should be central to this endeavor: "Not only does this provide an opportunity for tea to become international and worthy to be propagated the world over, but it provides the means by which Japan can become again an equal member of nations through Rikyu's philosophy of 'Harmony, Respect, Purity, and Tranquility.'"

The "peace treaty tea" was going to be held in conjunction with an exhibition of Japanese art at the San Francisco Golden Gate Museum. The treaty was for Hounsai an occasion "for the Japanese to grasp the true meaning of American democracy and to become international citizens and for Americans and other foreigners to abandon their sense of superiority and to fully understand the quality of Oriental art. . . . I strongly believe that all new Japanese citizens should carry tea in their hearts."

Though there was the usual difficulty presented by the lack of tatami (they made do with straw mats), Hounsai's tea went well. Daisetz Suzuki lectured on Zen and talked about Rikyu. They were a natural team, in a way, since Suzuki was also propagating Japanese spirituality, in the form of Zen, in the postwar period as an instrument to promote understanding of Japan and Japanese culture around the world.

Though Hounsai was resolutely optimistic, propagating the idea of tea and peace in the United States was not an easy task. He had three major obstacles to face. First, prejudices and even anti-Japanese hatred that had proliferated during the war had to be addressed. Anthropologist Ruth Benedict famously offered a solution to this problem with the theory of "the chrysanthemum and the sword," that

Japan had two opposite cultures, the sword of violence, represented by Japan's samurai culture and military aggression; and the chrysanthemum, a highly refined, aesthetic culture of peace. Hounsai firmly identified the tradition of tea with the latter: "Tea is hope, faith, and determination, as well as peace. This is the tradition of the Way of Tea and the intention of Sen Rikyu. It is only on the basis of these notions that the message of tea should be carried aboard."

Another obstacle Hounsai had to overcome was the American notion that tea was a kind of religion and its performance a kind of ceremony or prayer. Having attended Doshisha, Hounsai was aware of the religious services held in American Christian churches, and no doubt he understood the thinking that led to the association of tea with religion. Hounsai surmounted this obstacle by ignoring it; at any rate, it was an idea that he did little to dispel. After all, tea was Zen, and in his own personal experience, he saw little need to draw distinctions between religions.

The third obstacle Hounsai faced was at home: the typical Japanese sectarianism, which expressed itself in criticism of Hounsai's drive for the internationalization of tea by other tea schools. The tendency in Japan to "hit the nail that sticks out" fell full force on Hounsai. He was young, enthusiastic, and innovative. It was only to be expected that conservative elements of the tea world would oppose his efforts.

He remained undaunted, however, and responded by developing a carefully planned strategy for teaching tea abroad, seriously thought out step by step: "The environment in the United States is totally foreign to that which produced the Way of Tea, and it would have been wrong to think of propagating that spiritual practice as if it were export merchandise, like cameras."

After he returned home, the University of Hawaii offered Hounsai a position teaching tea at its evening adult school. Hounsai was excited: "Not even in Japan had tea ever been taught at the university level." He accepted, and as he was teaching his course, Hounsai also took regular daytime classes in literature, art, and American and world history.

Hounsai was fortunate to receive counsel and support from key figures in these years of activity overseas. Goto Roshi encouraged Hounsai to persevere in his course of action while at the same time complaining bitterly about his frequent foreign trips. Jokingly, he said that giving him the name Hounsai (Phoenix Cloud) did not mean that he should take wing so often.

> You should be more cautious and not spread your wings so far. But, on the other hand, it may very well be your task in life to travel about. Each grand tea master in the history of the Sen family has suffered the hardships of his age and I suppose you are meant to devote your life to these foreign pilgrimages. People such as yourself are, on the whole, blessed with good fortune from birth. You completed your education and experienced a war, and you should feel grateful for such a broad background. Your father

spread the Way of Tea to the entire nation. The important question is what
to do now that it is your turn.

With some reservations, Hounsai became a representative of traditional
Japanese culture overseas, and in that role he became increasingly involved in cultural diplomacy. In 1954, the city of São Paulo in Brazil asked Hounsai to serve tea
at the four-hundredth anniversary of the city's founding. The ceremony was to
honor at the same time the pioneering contributions of the local Japanese community to the city. For Hounsai this was an opportunity to introduce tea to the
"Land of Coffee." In Brazil, Hounsai learned about the experiences of many first-
generation Japanese Brazilians, and in a report back home writes with surprise and
admiration for the "Three Principles" cherished by Japanese immigrants: work all
year long; don't complain about food, clothing, or your dwelling for the first five
years; and whatever your job, do it and endure.

His semiofficial government assignments did not stop here. In 1965 the Ministry
of Foreign Affairs sent him to Rio de Janeiro to attend the four-hundredth anniver-
sary of that city. In the following year the ministry sent him to New York for the
Japan Art Fair, and in 1972 to Munich for the Cultural Events of the Olympic
Games. In 1976, he was to return to UNESCO as an official representative of the
Japanese government.

Hounsai traveled to Europe for the first time in 1958. The Japanese Embassy in
Brussels asked him to offer a tea demonstration in May, during the World Fair.
Prior to the demonstration, he stayed in Paris for several months, where he found
that Japanese art was held in a sufficiently high esteem for him to propagate tea in
France. As Japan recovered from the war, it became possible to ship precious tea
utensils abroad, allowing Hounsai to offer Westerners a more genuine tea and to
show off the finest works of Japanese art, and he arranged to have art and utensils
shipped to him for the Brussels demonstration. Unfortunately, it did not arrive in
time for the "Evening of Tea" at the Japanese Embassy in Brussels, and once again
improvisation was the order of the day.

Hounsai was also concerned about the poor quality of Europe's water at the
time. Kyoto, tea's birthplace, boasts many fine natural wells, one of which is in
the Urasenke compound. In June, Hounsai offered a tea demonstration at the
Japanese embassy in Paris, and another in mid-November to commemorate the
inauguration of the new UNESCO building, which had a sculpture garden
designed by Isamu Noguchi.

June 3, Hounsai was to offer tea on the occasion of an exhibition of Japanese art
in Paris. He was able to borrow the utensils he needed from the Musée Guimet.
The result was an astounding array of first-rate Japanese art:

Tokonoma alcove: Landscape painting by Sesshu, National Treasure
Ceramic tea container: Old Bizen, borrowed from the Musée Guimet

Flowers: Iris

Incense container: An old piece lacquered with design, once possessed by Queen Marie-Antoinette

Tray: Fan-shaped, once possessed by Queen Marie-Antoinette

Additional tokonoma alcove decoration: Box made of colored paper, favored by Tantansai

Kettle: Fujigama made by Seiemon

Kettle: Karakane shaped in the style of Jo'o

Water container: Karatsu in the shape of a water chestnut, borrowed from the Musée Guimet

Tea container for thin tea: San'yu Natsume favored by Tantansai

Tea scoop: Made by Tantansai and named "Bankoku no Tomo" (Peace on Earth)

Bowl: Made and painted by Ninsei, borrowed from the Musée Guimet

Other tea bowls: Various

Waste-water container: Made by Oribe, borrowed from the Musée Guimet

Lid rest: Metal, made in Paris

Cakes: Choseiden made by Morihachi and Yushin made by Suetomi

Cake trays: An old round tray and Kotobukibon favored by Tantansai

Tea: "Wa no Mukashi" manufactured by Ippodo

Water: From a well at Passy

Prominent members of the French government, professors, and diplomats attended the tea meeting, which was centered on Sesshu's painting. The celebrated Japanese painter Domoto Hisao was also among the guests.

On his way back to Japan, Hounsai stopped briefly in Athens. Looking at Greek ruins, he pondered about why the Japanese preserved tea in the absence of stone and marble buildings. His conclusion was that tea survived because it became part of the daily lives of the people. He also stopped over in Burma, serving tea at the Japanese embassy and the university in Rangoon.

Since he started on his internationalization drive, Hounsai has visited about fifty nations and traveled abroad about one hundred and seventy times. Hounsai has indeed made it his sacred mission to spread tea abroad and to this day, when many voices remind him of needs at home, he continues on this course with determination.

Marriage and Activities as Wakasosho

Busy with his duties both at home and abroad, Hounsai was now thirty years old. Pressure was mounting on him to get married to a suitable girl and secure the Urasenke succession. In 1954, when his father Tantansai had turned sixty, people wanted Hounsai to congratulate his father by announcing his engagement. His bride-to-be was Tomiko, the third daughter of a Tokyo textile wholesaler, and an accomplished speaker of French. The famous writer Yoshikawa Eiji was to be the go-between and the marriage ceremony was set for January 30, 1955. All of this had to be duly announced at the Urasenke ancestral shrine. Despite his international experience, Hounsai's honeymoon was restricted to a short trip to Kyushu. His busy schedule prevented him from taking a longer trip to a more distant destination.

As wakasosho, Hounsai had to fulfill a busy ritual schedule at home. This included offerings at the ancestral shrine at the anniversaries of the deaths of Rikyu, Sotan, Gengensai, and others, as well as the New Year's Tea. Later, as iemoto, he selected July 5 for the memorial services of Genegensai, Ennosai, and Mugensai. "There is a memorial service for one of my ancestors or some other important associate almost every day," he writes.[6]

Another important annual event is the reception of the new crop of fresh tea that the Kanbayashi family of tea growers brings in a Luson jar on November 19, and the formal cutting of the jar's mouth. There are in addition the daily observances at Urasenke, such as offerings to the local deity (*jishu-sama*) and the bodhisattva Jizo (Skt., Ksitigharba). One of the wife's main duties was to oversee the daily production or selection of tea sweets, as well as the preparation of tea food for formal meetings.

His international activities notwithstanding, Hounsai also strove to consolidate tea at home. Soon after the war, in 1948, he created the Seinenkai to promote tea among young people and to build the foundation for the next tea generation. Then he founded the Showakai. He joined the Rotary Club and the Lion's Club and several sports clubs, and his wife joined the Soroptimist International.

In 1962, Hounsai established a live-in college called Urasenke Gakuen, despite his predecessor's reservations about undertaking such a project. The first year's enrollment was ten female and ten male students. During the three-year curriculum, the student learned tea proceedings, preparation of the brazier or hearth in the winter, social manners and etiquette, the preparation of tea foods, and other general-education subjects, including English. Urasenke Gakuen students acquire the fundamentals of tea practice and tea philosophy and learn to evaluate the quality of tea and water. Now there are about thirty students, including fifteen foreign students, enrolled. A scholarship program to invite foreign students began also around that time. So far over five hundred foreign students have studied there as members of the so-called Midori-kai (Green Group).

The Death of Tantansai

Hounsai's grandfather Ennosai had died suddenly while teaching during a special summer course. Tantansai, Hounsai's father, also died unexpectedly, on September

7, 1964, during a lecture tour in Hokkaido. He was seventy-one. In his autobiography, Hounsai wrote about his father:

> Tantansai destroyed his health for the sake of tea. He did not seek honors, enjoyed tea in all things, and dedicated himself fully to the propagation of tea. He lived up to his reputation of being a true tea man. . . . He had a strong personality with a powerful mind and a posture that reflected his virtues and good heart. He virtually lived tea.

Even after Tantansai's death, Hounsai looked up to his father as his ideal. Twenty-three years after, Hounsai wrote the following about his father:

> Tantansai was everything he should have been. It may seem unreserved of me to say this of my own father, but I am not alone in this opinion. People who knew him—even, for instance, persons affiliated with other schools of tea—often tell me he was a true man of tea. . . . He had a commanding character befitting a grand tea master. Whenever I hear such words of praise about my father, I reflect upon myself and feel very inadequate.[7]

Upon receiving the news of Tantansai's death, Hounsai immediately flew to Hokkaido to bring his father's body back to Kyoto. All Urasenke family members gathered and, during the night-long vigil, Tantansai's younger brother Iguchi Kaisen announced in a loud voice, "I declare Hounsai Soko as the next grand master. Is there anybody in this assembly who objects?" As nobody objected, Okazaki Shigeyuki declared, "There are no objections. We are all united in accepting your new leadership." With that, Hounsai became the new grand master, the fifteenth descendant of Sen Rikyu. He relates his feelings at the time: "I was thus appointed new grand master by universal acclaim. However, I felt forlorn. My father has been a truly great master. Although I had already reached the age of forty-one, losing my father was like a flame blown out in front of my eyes. I honestly did not feel up to the job."

IEMOTO

It was not just the loss of his father that weighed on Hounsai's mind. There were also all the funeral arrangements and the inheritance formalities, as well as a change of name from Soko to Soshitsu. The legal formalities in changing his name were overwhelming. In May the following year, Hounsai had to vow in front of the ancestral shrine to fulfill all the grand master's obligations. The subsequent offertory tea at the Heian Shrine was his first as iemoto.

Hounsai soon settled into his role. "Because I served as wakasosho close to my father for fourteen years," he writes, "tea had sufficiently become a part of myself.

Therefore I felt comfortable with my new role fairly quickly." As the new grand tea master, Hounsai once more formulated his tea philosophy: "This is my principle: It is culture that determines the rise and fall of peoples and not military might. . . . Japan's postwar success is a victory of the people and proof that violence does not bring about a people's victory; it is their culture that allows them to survive." For Hounsai, tea is a sort of victory in the struggle for social cohesiveness that one finds in all cultures. Yet culture also serves in fostering international understanding, and this is why all peoples, including the Japanese, must be aware of and actively practice and contribute to their own culture. When culture is open and egalitarian, like Tantansai's and Hounsai's tea, it is an export of peace.

Yet there were many things close to home that Hounsai still did not know. For example, only the grand masters have access to the Urasenke storehouse and the right to withdraw utensils to be used in tea meetings. Tantansai had kept meticulous records of his entries into the storehouse and Hounsai had to learn where all the precious utensils were stored. He also had to perform the traditional duty of the grand master to sign the box lids of tea utensils. In addition, he had to assume the leadership of numerous associates and tea people around Japan. He became painfully aware that despite all his training there were still areas in which he had not yet achieved complete expertise. He describes his feelings at the time: "I was forced to take care of everything myself and, despite the warmth of my mother, my wife, and my family, I was overcome by an unprecedented feeling of loneliness."

The time had come for Hounsai to move into his father's quarters, which were extremely plain. The real treasures of Urasenke are the tea rooms past grand masters have built, all of which the Japanese government has designated Important Cultural Properties: Sotan's Konnichian, Yuin, and Kan'untei; Gengensai's Totsutotsusai, Hosensai, and Ryuseiken; and Ennosai's Tairyuken. "The place where I live," wrote Hounsai, "is unlike these tea rooms. These are the quarters that were built when my father got married." The only "luxuries" there were the plum trees and bamboo grove. Tantansai's personal quarters were over seventy years old, and only recently has air conditioning been installed in the guest room. They are hot in summer and cold in winter. Many a friend who visited these living quarters was shocked and suggested tearing them down immediately and building something more modern. Hounsai, however, has not done so; he subscribes to Rikyu's advice that a house is good enough if it does not leak.

After he gets up at five-thirty each morning, Hounsai first offers prayers and a bowl of tea at the ancestral chapel, before he proceeds to the shrine of the local deity in the garden to offer prayers. Then he opens the storehouse to select the utensils to be used that day and goes to the tea rooms to inspect the flower arrangements and the fires. At seven o'clock he eats breakfast. After that he checks his schedule and, shortly before nine, exchanges greetings with his entire staff. But this is just the beginning of Hounsai's daily routine. He has no vacations, days off, or leisurely Sundays. His schedule is filled with the visits of guests, offering tea at temples and shrines, attending tea meetings at Urasenke branches all over the country, and with about six or seven trips abroad each year. The New Year season is especially busy because he has to host tea meetings every day and serve tea, food, and saké to thousands of tea practitioners assembling at Urasenke.

According to Urasenke custom, all the grand master's brothers and sisters must assume different family names. Hounsai's uncle assumed the name Iguchi, and his own brother Yoshiharu, the name Naya—in reference to the Nayashu, a Sakai group to which Rikyu's family had belonged. Yoshiharu first wanted to study medicine (Sotan's son Senso had studied Chinese medicine before he was called back to tea by his father), but he gave up and instead founded a publishing company that publishes books and journals on tea. The monthly journal *Tanko* that it publishes is an outgrowth of Ennosai's *Konnichian Geppo*. Hounsai's elder sister Shiotsuki Yaeko also involves herself in tea, publishes on tea, and teaches tea at various schools.

In spite of his duties as grand master, Hounsai continued his international drive. It had become customary for Japan's official guests to drink a bowl of tea at Urasenke. Hounsai and his wife were adept at explaining tea in English or French. In 1975, he offered tea to Queen Elizabeth II at the Katsura Imperial Villa on the outskirts of Kyoto, serving her and the Duke of Edinburgh on a misonodana table with a tea scoop named Lady of the Lake, made the year before by the British poet Sir Edmund Blunden. Another tea scoop, by Emperor Kokaku (1771–1840), was displayed. The bowl was made by Raku Kichizaemon and named "Kiun" (Happy Cloud). One of the tea containers and the water jar had been made by Eiraku Zengoro, and the thin tea container with a phoenix design was made by Sotetsu. In November 1979, Hounsai served tea to Deng Xiaoping of China; to President Mitterrand and his wife Danielle in 1982; and to King Phumiphol of Thailand in January 1986. In 1992, he served tea to Mikhail and Raisa Gorbachev in Kyoto and in August 1995 to Richard von Weiszäcker, former president of Germany. After hearing Hounsai's explanation of Gengensai's calligraphic *"Wa, Kei, Sei, Jaku,"* von Weizsäcker praised Hounsai for his efforts for peace on the basis of traditional culture. Hounsai served tea in the "Toyama" tea bowl made by Tantansai and explained to von Weizsäcker that "Toyama" derived from the Zen saying, "The distant mountains, layers upon layers of blue, stretch out endlessly."

Hounsai also continued to promote tea at foreign universities and traveled abroad as a cultural ambassador of Japan. Under its Distinguished Guest Program, the University of Hawaii offered him a post teaching a yearly seminar on tea. Since 1966, he has never missed a single seminar. In 1969 he traveled to Egypt and to Cologne to inaugurate the Japan-German Cultural Center and to inaugurate a new tea hut in the Bois de Boulogne in Paris. In 1970 he revisited Brazil at the behest of the Foreign Ministry to inaugurate the Japan House in São Paulo. In the same year, the government of Portugal appointed him Honorary Consul. In 1973, he went to Australia to lecture on tea at Queensland University, and in 1974, he offered tea at the New York Japan House Gallery to inaugurate a year-long exhibition on tea art. In 1981, Hounsai created a school and factory in Thailand to provide work in the refugee camps and to try to preserve the Laotian weaving traditions. In the spring of that year, Hounsai went to New York to inaugurate the new Chanoyu Center in New York. While there, he was asked how was it that tea is able to contribute so much to life. Hounsai replied, stressing that tea is a way of self-discovery that one can only attain through some form or discipline:

> Chanoyu is, of course, much more than the preparation of tea. It is a way of life, applicable anywhere by anyone. To understand this centuries-old discipline we must first look deeply into the outward forms of chanoyu, and then look beyond them. Only then can one see that the foundation of chanoyu is mind—our own mind—and spirit—our own spirit. It is this realization that suggests to us that the life of tea is, in fact, the same as the life we lead every day. The realization that a life predicated on the four principles of the Way of Tea—"harmony, respect, purity, tranquility"—is a rich and rewarding life grows out of the practice of chanoyu. This is how chanoyu can contribute so much to life.[8]

Based on the Japanese tradition of tea as an offering to the Shinto and Buddhist deities, Hounsai also started to offer tea at Christian churches in Guam, New York, and Rome. At the invitation of Pope John Paul II, Hounsai traveled to Rome in December 1984 to offer tea at the Vatican. He stopped over in Copenhagen only to find out that Alitalia had gone on strike. He and his wife then flew to Geneva and from there were taken on an Italian military jet to Rome, just in time for a mass at San Angelmo. This offertory tea in a Catholic church was an important moment in Hounsai's international drive. He wrote the following about his experience:

> I had not discussed anything about the procedures for serving tea with the papal representative beforehand. I commenced the *otemae* to the side of the altar as he began the service, made tea, and carried it to the altar. There, as if he had planned it, the priest had completed a purification ritual and, without a moment of awkwardness, stood ready to receive the bowl of tea I proffered. It was a symbolic moment, I felt, in which the cultures of East and West were neatly knit into one.[9]

Hounsai's lecture on tea at the Papal Reception Hall after the offertory tea was attended by several thousand listeners.

In June 1995 Hounsai went to see the grottoes of Dunhuang, one of the masterpieces of East Asian Buddhist art. This was the start of the ongoing friendship between Urasenke and the People's Republic of China and, ironically perhaps, of the export of tea back to China, where the tradition of tea has completely vanished for many reasons.

A visit to Moscow, too, offered Hounsai the opportunity to demonstrate what he had come to call his "Tea of Peacefulness." In August 1988 Hounsai traveled there to offer tea as part of the celebration of the establishment of Japanese-Soviet cooperation. The Gorbachevs were not there, but Hounsai had the opportunity to see how the Soviet Union was changing under Gorbachev's leadership. He also offered tea at the Danilov Monastery on the occasion of the first millennial anniversary of the establishment of the Russian Orthodox church. "Overcoming religious and national differences," Hounsai wrote, "I felt great joy to offer a bowl of tea as a prayer for peace to the Soviet people."[10]

Hounsai also helped in establishing courses on tea at U.S. universities other than Hawaii, including the University of California at Berkeley, the University of Washington in Seattle, and the University of California at Los Angeles. In September 1983, he visited Beijing to inaugurate a chair of tea at Beijing University. In 1986, he donated one million dollars to the University of Hawaii for the creation of a Hounsai Chair. Under the motto "A Bowl of Peacefulness," Hounsai makes a trip each year to lecture at the university, which awarded him the title of professor in 1980.

To spread the message of tea abroad, Hounsai launched the journal *Chanoyu Quarterly* in 1970, a biannual English publication about tea. This coincided with the establishment of the Midorikai, the earlier mentioned group of foreign students invited each year to spend a year of study and practice at Urasenke, mostly based on scholarships provided by Urasenke.

In 1984, economic frictions between Japan and the Western nations had intensified to the extent of undermining the very principles of postwar international relations. At that time, Hounsai advised his countrymen not to export and enrich themselves more and more, but to drink tea and study their own traditional culture. Reflecting on the future of international economic relationships and in his own unique way anticipating the economic changes that the information revolution would cause, he remarked that Japan should export culture instead of material goods.

Hounsai's international tea was also directed toward home; it helped him to better define tea and to dispel criticisms and misconceptions of tea in Japan as well as to discover cultural similarities between Japan and other nations. It also helped him to remind his countrymen to cultivate their own culture. For him, that was the only guarantee for peace. In his writings, Hounsai identifies the green color of the tea with the green of peace. The scope of Hounsai's understanding of the universal meaning of tea appears perhaps best of all in the following statement: "East is east, and west is west, Kipling insisted, but this is no longer so. East is west and west is east."[11]

Young Japanese were of course more receptive to Hounsai's internationalization of tea, and he realized that his drive would not survive without educating the young: "We need to educate people who can communicate internationally. Just knowing a foreign language or a foreign country does not make one eligible to be called international." For Hounsai, to be international meant to know well one's culture and traditions: "A true international Japanese is also a true Japanese."[12] Hounsai therefore emphasized the need to educate the Japanese in their own culture. With this in mind, in 1973 he organized a nationwide gathering in which two thousand eight hundred young tea people participated. He told them to never lose the ability to reflect and to improve themselves. Some of these associations have established contacts with similar groups abroad. In June 1974, for the first time he rented a passenger ship taking young Japanese tea people abroad. In July 1977 he took them to Hong Kong and in July 1980 to China.

One day in 1983 Hounsai's son Masayuki told his father he wanted to speak to him in private. He revealed that he was dating Princess Masako, the daughter of Prince Mikasa, Emperor Hirohito's (known since his death as Emperor Showa) younger brother, and that he wanted to get married. Both families having agreed to the marriage, permission had to be obtained from the Imperial Household Agency and the Cabinet. Once these hurdles were overcome, the marriage ceremony was set for October 14. In the case of marriage with a member of the imperial family, there is no need for a go-between, and in June the formal gifts (tokens of engagement) were exchanged. In September the emperor was informed. The marriage ceremony took place in the Totsutotsai room at Urasenke followed by a party at the Heian Shrine.

Masako is learning the roles of the grand master's wife and has adapted well to the Urasenke family. On November 10, 1984, Akifumi, the next heir of Urasenke was born, and in 1987, a daughter, Makiko. On July 6, 1990 a second son, Takafumi, was born. Masakazu, Hounsai's second son (born in 1958) also married and fathered two sons. For the time being, Urasenke succession into the twenty-first century is secure.

Hounsai has established Urasenke branches and supporting groups in more than twenty countries. Hounsai sent twenty Urasenke teachers to teach in thirteen countries. In the United States alone, there are twelve branches with five Urasenke-trained teachers. In Japan there are one hundred sixty-seven branches. Hounsai visits these branches at important occasions and anniversaries.

Hounsai has received countless awards, honors, and decorations from various governments. Brazil, Finland, France, Germany, Italy, Peru, and Thailand have honored him for his contributions to the understanding of Japanese culture. In 1983, the University of Hawaii awarded him an honorary doctorate. He had already received an honorary doctorate from Seton Hall in 1976 on the basis of a dissertation he wrote on the *Cha Jing*, the Chinese "Book of Tea." Based on his studies of tea before Rikyu, especially tea in China, he received a doctorate from Nanguan University in the People's Republic of China. Moscow University also honored him with an honorary degree.

At home, too, Hounsai has become one of the most honored citizens. The emperor awarded him the Medal of Honor with Blue Ribbon eight times and in 1994, the Order of the Rising Sun, Second Class. In 1989 he was named Person of Cultural Merit, and in 1995 he received the Japan Foundation Award and the Foreign Minister's Commendation. In November 1997 came his highest award, the Emperor's Medal of Culture, in recognition of his contributions to and leadership in Japanese traditional culture. This award was bestowed on Hounsai both as an individual and as an institution.

part three

Hounsai as an Arbiter of Taste

Hounsai Konomimono

Ever since the iemoto system was put into place, one of the iemoto's important duties and means of expressing artistic authority has been in designing or sponsoring the design of tea utensils. This is a major way in which each iemoto defines the tea of his generation. Grand masters often entrusted the design of a new utensil to one of the Ten Artisans of the Sen Family (Senke Jusshoku), craftsman families traditionally linked to the Senke. In return for the patronage of the Senke, the craftsmen of the ten families promised not to reproduce the especially commissioned designs without the consent of the iemoto. The reason for this is simple: when the iemoto gives away a utensil designed to his taste to an important guest, he symbolically gives part of himself, represented by the exclusive design called a "liking" or "taste" (konomi). If the utensil were available from another source, it could not represent the unique authority of the iemoto.

Precedent requires that a utensil designed or favored by the iemoto, known as his *konomimono*, must be displayed on certain occasions, such as the anniversary of Rikyu's death, Sotan's death, the visit of important guests, the birth of an heir, or other such auspicious events. Of course the iemoto, Hounsai included, may also use konomimono on other occasions as well.

In the following discussion we shall examine some of the most successful designs sponsored by Hounsai. The degree of the iemoto's participation in the design and production process varies according to the object. He may merely give the craftsman general guidelines, but in the cases of calligraphy and tea scoops, the iemoto himself does the writing or the carving. For tables (daisu), tea huts, gardens, tea caddies, and other more complicated or specialized utensils, the iemoto entrusts the entire design and manufacture to one of his craftsmen, though he approves the work at various stages. An iemoto may also sponsor the work of an artist or artisan outside the jusshoku system.

141

Teahuts and Tea Rooms

Since he became Urasenke iemoto, Hounsai has built over twenty teahuts in Japan and over fifteen abroad. In designing these huts, Hounsai was particularly concerned about how they fit into their natural environment. Whether at Ise Shrine or at Himeji Castle, these huts have been built at sites that the Japanese government has designated an Important Cultural Property or UNESCO has designated as part of our World Cultural Heritage.

HOSHOAN

Hoshoan teahut, designed by Hounsai and built in 1967 with a donation from Matsushita Konosuke. Set in the gardens of the International Conference Hall in northern Kyoto, it contains a ten-mat room and a ryurei (Western-style) room. The ryurei is a copy of the Yushin room designed by Tantansai at Urasenke. The hut has a roof thatched with cypress bark.

Carpenter: Nakamura Sotoji
Garden Designer: Kawasaki Kojiro

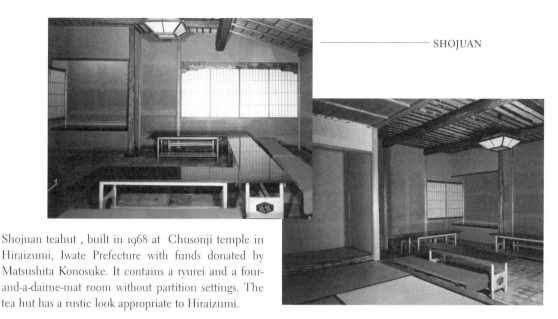

SHOJUAN

HOSHOAN

Shojuan teahut , built in 1968 at Chusonji temple in Hiraizumi, Iwate Prefecture with funds donated by Matsushita Konosuke. It contains a ryurei and a four-and-a-daime-mat room without partition settings. The tea hut has a rustic look appropriate to Hiraizumi.

Carpenter: Nakamura Sotoji
Garden Designer: Iwaki Sentaro

Hoshoan teahut, built in 1969 in the Nishinomaru Garden of Osaka Castle as Matsushita Konosuke's gift to the city of Osaka. The *ho* of Hoshoan can also be read as the *toyo* of Toyotomi Hideyoshi, who built the castle, and *sho* (pine) can also be read *matsu*, as in the name of sponsor Matsushita Konosuke. It has a large reception room, a four-and-one-half-mat room, and a ryurei room, each provided with its own kitchen (*mizuya*). The roji path leading up to the four-and-one-half-mat room is particularly well designed.

Carpenter: Nakamura Sotoji
Garden Designer: Kawasaki Kojiro

ISE SHRINE

Teahut at the Ise Shrine (Naiku), donated by Matsushita Konosuke. It was built in 1985 to entertain important guests. It has a ten-mat room (Ichinoma), a nine-mat room (Ninoma), a six-and-one-half-mat room (Tsuginoma) with a three-mat higher-level room, and another ten-mat room with a higher-level five-mat room. This arrangement is reminiscent of the reception rooms (*kaisho*) of the Ashikaga shoguns. The latter ten-mat room is built over a pond. At the northern end of the complex, there is a four-and-one-half-mat room with a nijiriguchi and a roji.

Carpenter: Nakamura Sotoji
Garden Designer: Iwaki Sentaro

SOJUAN

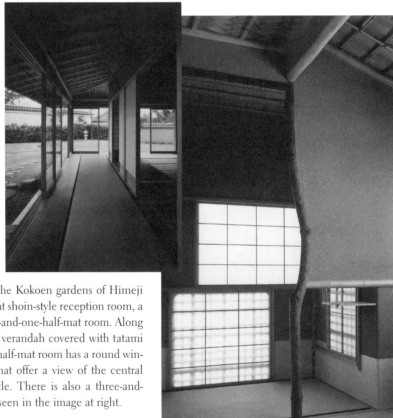

Sojuan teahut, built in the Kokoen gardens of Himeji Castle. It has an eight-mat shoin-style reception room, a six-mat room, and a four-and-one-half-mat room. Along the reception rooms is a verandah covered with tatami mats. The four-and-one-half-mat room has a round window and sliding doors that offer a view of the central building of Himeji Castle. There is also a three-and-one-daime-mat room as seen in the image at right.

Carpenter: Miyake Tsutomu
Garden Designer: Ogawa Masayuki

Built in 1993, the Todoken teahut is owned by the Ohi family of Kanazawa. It contains an eight-mat and a six-mat reception room and a two-and-a-daime-mat small room. This hut is reminiscent of the "mountain huts" built in the cities in the sixteenth century. Here we see the temaeza of the small room with its natural post.

Carpenter: Maeda Shizuka
Garden Designer: Uemura Akihide

——————————————— URASENKE TOKYO CENTER

Urasenke Tokyo Center, built in 1995. Baian's temaeza (right) and roji leading to the Totsutotsusai tea room (above).

Carpenters: Maeda Shizuka, Onuma Toyofumi
Garden Designer: Iwaki Shojiro

SHOUN'AN————————

Shoun'an teahouse. This nineteenth-century stable in New York City was refurbished in 1981 to become the New York Urasenke Chanoyu Center. It has an inner garden and an eight-mat, a ten-mat, and a four-and-one-half-mat small room as well as a seven-mat waiting room.
(above) Front view
(left) Roji, waiting parlor, and entrance.

Carpenter: Ueno Nobuhiro
Garden Designer: Kato Saburo

SEIKOAN ————————————

Seikoan teahut at the Japanese Cultural Center of Hawaii. The original Seikoan was a small hut having only a six-mat and a three-and-one-daime-mat room. The present one has an eight-mat room, a ryurei room, and a three-and-one-daime-mat room. The hut successfully integrates the Hawaiian building code into a traditional Japanese teahut. It is surrounded by typical Hawaiian vegetation arranged in the manner of a Japanese garden.
(above) Front dry landscape garden
(below) Eight-mat Hiroma room and ryurei.

Carpenter: Suzuki Kazuyuki
Garden Designer: Kiyohara Sekimizu

RAIJUAN

Raijuan, built in 1989 at the Royal Museum of History and Art in Brussels, Belgium. It was built when Japan was chosen as the guest nation at the Exhibition Europalia. The teahut, consisting of a four-and-one-half-mat room, stands as a separate building in one of the museum halls.

Carpenter: Miyake Tsutomu

Food

On October 5, 1990 Hounsai hosted a tea party at the four-hundredth anniversary of Rikyu's death and invited Sen Sosa, the head of the Omote Senke school, and other tea people. What we see here is part of the food he offered: (left) fried butterfish, (center) fish eggs with thinly sliced squid, and (right) dried mullet roe with salt-fried yam.

Kettles

Kettle on brazier, Korean style, made by fifteenth-generation Senke Jusshoku kettle maker Onishi Joshin. It bears the name "Hoo Jimon Shinnarigama," meaning Phoenix Kettle. Cast on its surface are Chinese mythical animals such as the phoenix, *kirin*, a turtle, and the dragon. This kettle was made on the occasion of Hounsai's seventieth birthday in 1994.

This cone-shaped kettle was cast by sixteenth-generation Onishi Seiemon. It has a design of pines and bamboo along a stream. The ears and lid handle are in the form of pine cones. The kettle imparts the impression of a river widening as it flows away from its source. The tripod brazier is made of copper. It has a moon-shaped vent. This was made on the theme "Uninterrupted Flow of Water" for the Urasenke exhibition of paintings on the beauties of nature and for Hounsai's seventieth birthday.

This gourd-shaped kettle was cast by thirteenth-generation Miyazaki Kanchi. 1983 konomimono.

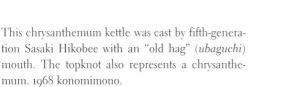

This chrysanthemum kettle was cast by fifth-generation Sasaki Hikobee with an "old hag" (*ubaguchi*) mouth. The topknot also represents a chrysanthemum. 1968 konomimono.

Incense Containers

This bamboo incense container shaped as a crescent moon is called "Akigusa-e Tsuki Kogo" and has a design of autumn grasses. It reminds one of the moon rising above the mountaintops. It was made by thirteenth-generation Kuroda Shogen and is a 1977 Hounsai konomimono.

Water Jars

This water jar was made by sixteenth-generation Eiraku Zengoro commemorating the Year of the Horse (1990), one of the Chinese zodiacal signs. The heavenly horse is painted inside a ginkgo leaf. Other designs are pines, bamboo, and white and red plums. The lid handle has the shape of a plum blossom bud.

Red raku water jar shaped by Hounsai and fired by Raku Kichizaemon.

Mishima water jar made by tenth-generation Ohi Chozaemon from the red clay found in Ohi village, Ishikawa Prefecture. This jar was baked three times to obtain the desired color, a technique that earned the potter the Commendation of the Arts Council. 1994 konomimono.

Tea Caddies

This seven-sided caddy was made by thirteenth-generation Kuroda Shogen at the occasion of Hounsai's seventieth birthday in 1994 and named "Kinrinji." The model for this is a container now at the temple Daiun'in. The lid hangs down over the edge. Lacquered bamboo.

Made by twelfth-generation Nakamura Sotetsu, this elongated container is called "Tarumi" (Waterfall) and reminds one of water swiftly falling over a rock into a river below. This is part of a series of four containers designed on the theme of the beauties of nature. The container represents summer coolness. Konomimono of 1994.

Large tea caddy made by Takagi Gyokuei and named "Saikan" (Colored Circle). 1965 konomimono.

Tea caddy with design representing all the traditional treasures, made by ninth-generation Ogura Sakon. 1992 konomimono.

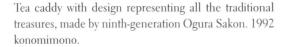

Tea container "Benzaiten," one of seven containers representing the Seven Gods of Good Fortune, Daikokuten, Ebisu, Bishamonten, Benzaiten, Fukurokuju, Jurojin, and Hotei. Benzaiten is the only female deity among the seven. Made in 1965 by third-generation Suzuki Hyosaku..

"Hotei," made by third-generation Suzuki Hyosaku.

Tea caddy representing a rice-straw bag made by third-generation Suzuki Hyosaku. 1994 konomimono.

Trays

This seven-sided tray (kotobukibon) was made by Komazawa Risai. This phoenix design has been a trademark of the Komazawa family for generations. The dancing phoenix assumes the shape of a cloud. It was made for Hounsai's seventieth birthday.

This tobacco box was made by twelfth-generation Tsuchida Yuko in the shape of an auspicious purple cloud. These colors represent the Heian period, the twelve-hundred-year anniversary of which was being celebrated in 1994, also the occasion of Hounsai's seventieth birthday.

Tea Bowls

Black tea bowl shaped by Hounsai and fired by Raku Kakunyu, named "Kokin" (Now and Then).

Red tea bowl shaped by Hounsai and fired by Raku Kakunyu, named "Shosei" (Voice of the Pine [Wind]).

White Raku tea bowl shaped by Hounsai and fired by
Raku Kichizaemon, named "Seiitsu" (Pure Pleasure).

Copy of the tea bowl "Hijiri" (Saint) made by ninth-
generation Ohi Chozaemon. Hounsai added the carvings.

Tea bowl by Ohi Chozaemon with a design of Mount
Fuji by Hounsai.

Tea bowl shaped and fired by Raku Chozaemon and
named "Ippuku" (A Sip).

Flower Vases

Made in imitation of Rikyu's bamboo vase by thir-teenth-generation Kuroda Shogen from a bamboo growing near the Konnichian complex. The inscription is by Hounsai.

Woven bamboo flower vase made by first-generation Tanaka Kosai. A 1968 konomimono.

Calligraphy

Calligraphy by Hounsai, "Where There Is Snow, There Are Plum Blossoms."

Calligraphy by Hounsai, "A Blossom Becomes Five Leaves."

Calligraphy by Hounsai, "A Stream Cannot Be Halted." Hounsai thought that this calligraphy suited the impression he once got when offering tea at the Kibune Shrine in northern Kyoto, which enshrines a water deity. "As the rapid, limpid river continued flowing, I thought how appropriate the saying: 'A stream cannot be halted.'"

Tea Scoops

Bamboo tea scoop carved by Hounsai during World War II and named "Wakazakura" (Young Cherry).

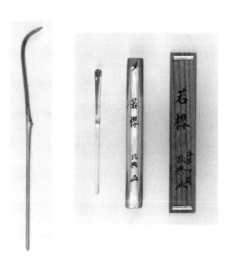

Bamboo tea scoop fashioned by Hounsai and named "Matsu Kokin Nashi" (Pines are Forever).

Bamboo tea scoop fashioned by Hounsai and named "Rokkasen" (The Six Immortal Poets).

Bamboo tea scoop carved by Hounsai and named "Shichifukujin" (The Seven Gods of Good Fortune).

Standing Screens (*furosaki*)

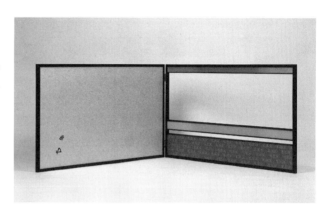

"Early Morning Cloud" standing screen made by Shunpodo with a "fresh grasses" motif on the lower panel. Konomimono of 1970.

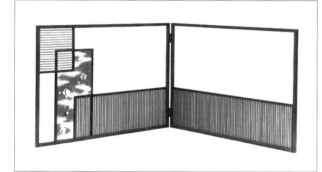

"Cloudy Moon" standing screen made by first-generation Hagii Kosai. Partly latticed. The golden sand represents clouds. 1965 konomimono.

Hearth Frames

Hearth frame with a design of Miwa Shrine, done by Iida Koshu. Hounsai offers tea every year on April 29 to the shrine. 1978 konomimono.

Tables (Stands)

"Mountain Cloud" stand made from cypress wood by third-generation Iwaki Shusai. The fifteen clouds represent the fifteen generations of Urasenke iemoto. A running stream design can be seen at two places. 1965 konomimono

Lid Rests

Lid rest in the shape of ginkgo leaves, made by thirteenth-generation Miyazaki Kanchi in reference to a ginkgo tree planted by Sotan. 1996 konomimono.

notes

Notes

INTRODUCTION

1. Reflecting the complexity of naming in Japanese traditional culture, I have chosen to use two different names in referring to Hounsai, first his childhood name Masaoki and then his Buddhist name Hounsai, which he carried as *wakasosho* or heir-designate, and later, as grand master (*iemoto*). From the time that he assumed the headship of the Urasenke School of Tea, the grand master used his official name Soshitsu Sen. This, however, is not a unique personal name, but the name that all his predecessors have used since Sotan's son Soshitsu founded the Urasenke school. I therefore prefer to use his unique Buddhist name Hounsai.

2. Sen Soshitsu, *Cha no Shintai* (Kyoto: Tankosha, 1983), 222–30.

3. Sen Soshitsu, "*Nijiriguchi no Imi*," Tanko 52, no. 5 (May 1998), 23.

4. In the summer, the shozumi occurs after the meal.

5. Such a tea meeting is described in Sen Soshitsu, *Tea Life, Tea Mind* (New York and Tokyo: Weatherhill, 1979), 27–30.

TEA AS PHILOSOPHY

1. *Cha no Shintai*, 230–31.

2. Taoists believe that there is more than one spirit in the body.

3. *Gunsho Ruiju*, vol. 9, Shosokubu (Tokyo: Zoku Gunsho Ruiju Kankokai, 1928), 712–13.

4. See Anna Seidel, *Taoismus: die inoffizielle Hochreligion Chinas*, OAG Aktuell 41, Deutsche Gesellschaft für Natur– und Volkerkunde Ostasiens (1990): 11.

5. *Chado Koten Zenshu*, vol. 1 (Kyoto: Tankosha, 1956), 20. For Lu Yu as the "God of Tea" see page 155.

6. Sen Soshitsu, *"Chakei" to Wagakuni Chado no Rekishiteki Igi* (Kyoto: Tankosha, 1983), 34.

7. The idea of one element "giving birth" to another stems from Dong Zhongshuo (176–104 BCE) in his *Chungqiu Fanlu*. The idea of "overcoming" was introduced by Zuo Qiuming, a contemporary of Confucius (551–479 BCE), who wrote the *Chungqiu Zuozhuan*.

8. There is a differing Indian classification based on the Four Basic Elements of Buddhism: earth, water, fire, and wind (or sky or void). See Sen, *"Chakei,"* 99.

9. *Shintei Zoho Kokushi Taikei*, vol. 32 (Tokyo: Yoshikawa Kobunkan, 1932), 709.

10. Doyo correspond to the four periods of transition between seasons. Special food is served in tea at such "in-between" seasons.

11. *Chado Koten Zenshu*, vol. 2 (Kyoto: Tankosha, 1956), 5–7. See also Hounsai's interpretation of these passages in *"Chakei,"* 86-87.

12. *Chado Koten Zenshu*, vol. 1, 346.

13. Ibid., 8–9.

14. Ibid., 264.

15. Gengensai Soshitsu, *Gengensai Chasho*, vol. 1, undated facsimile reprint (Kyoto: Konnichian), 43.

16. See Yoshino Hiroko, "The *I-ching* and Chanoyu," *Chanoyu Quarterly* 65 (1991), 19.

17. *Cha no Shintai*, 78–79.

18. Sen Soshitsu, "Chado to Inyo Gogyo," *Tanko* 51, no. 5 (May 1997), 23.

19. Sen Soshitsu, "The Implications of the Fukusa," *Chanoyu Quarterly* 65 (1991), 6–7.

20. Sen Soshitsu, "The Master in Ourselves," *Chanoyu Quarterly* 17 (1977), 6.

21. *Chado Koten Zenshu*, vol. 6 (Kyoto: Tankosha, 1956), 95.

22. *Chado Koten Zenshu*, vol. 4 (Kyoto: Tankosha, 1956), 3.

23. *Chado Koten Zenshu*, vol. 10 (Kyoto: Tankosha, 1956), 279–80.

24. Ibid., 279.

25. Ibid., 288.

26. Ibid., 292.

27. Ibid., 289.

28. Ibid., 303.

29. Michael Cooper, "The Early Europeans and Tea," H. Paul Varley, et. al., eds., *Tea in Japan: Essays on the History of Chanoyu* (Honolulu: University of Hawaii Press, 1989), 125.

30. Ibid., 235.

31. Sen, *Tea Life, Tea Mind*, 179, 60. The Rinzai school of Zen was introduced into Japan by Eisai.

32. Sen Soshitsu, "Understanding Chanoyu," *Chanoyu Quarterly* 1, no. 1 (Spring 1970) 6–7.

33. Hounsai adopts the Buddhist position here in including mind among the senses or perceptions.
34. Sen Soshitsu, "The Taste of Tea," *Chanoyu Quarterly* 25 (1980), 5.
35. Hamamoto Soshun, "A Tea Master's Vision of the Ten Oxherding Pictures," *Chanoyu Quarterly* 37 (1984), 39.
36. Sen Soshitsu, "One Time, One Meeting," *Chanoyu Quarterly* 49 (1987), 5–6.

TEA AS AN AESTHETIC

1. Sen Soshitsu, "Selfless Action," *Chanoyu Quarterly* 36 (1983), 5–6.
2. *Chado Koten Zenshu*, vol. 10, 296–97.
3. Ibid., 297.
4. *Chado Koten Zenshu*, vol. 3 (Kyoto: Tankosha, 1956), 51.
5. Quoted in the *Yamanoue Soji Ki*, in *Chado Koten Zenshu*, vol. 6, 101.
6. *Cha no Hon, The Book of Tea*, with a prologue and introduction by Soshitsu Sen (Tokyo: Kodansha International, Ltd., 1998), 35.
7. Donald Keene, trans., *Anthology of Japanese Literature: From the Earliest Era to the Mid-nineteenth Century* (New York: Grove Press, 1955), 239. Also in Donald Keene, trans., *Essays in Idleness*, (New York and London: Columbia University Press, 1967), 115–21.
8. *Chado Koten Zenshu*, vol. 4, 10.
9. Ibid., 16.
10. Ibid., 16–17.
11. Ibid.
12. Ibid., 17.
13. Quoted by Noh actor Konparu Zenpo in *Zenpo Zodan*, section 4, printed in *Kodai Chusei Geijutsuron, Nihon Shiso Taikei*, vol. 23 (Tokyo: Iwanami Shoten, 1973), 480.
14. Sen Soshitsu, "A Withered Tree Flowering," *Chanoyu Quarterly* 63 (1990), 6.
15. Ibid.
16. Ibid.

THE WAY OF TEA AND THE IEMOTO SYSTEM

1. *Wakan Chashi Yakuhon* (Osaka: privately published by Takaya Kotaro, 1914), 8–9. *Sukiya* here means "hut of a tea devotee." According to this source, it was Juko, not Rikyu, who was the true father of tea (see pages 34–35).
2. *Chado Koten Zenshu*, vol. 3, 3. Furuichi Harima (1459–1508) practiced "bath tea,"—enjoying tea after a bath. He later became the priest of the temple Kofukuji in Nara.
3. *Sogi Shogaku Sho*, quoted in Eto Yasusada, *Sogi no Kenkyu* (Tokyo: Kazama

Shobo, 1967), 429.

4. *Chado Koten Zenshu*, vol. 3, 3.

5. Ibid., 51.

6. See "Sanetaka, Jo'o, and *Iemoto Seido*," *Literary Patronage in Late Medieval Japan*, ed. by Steven D. Carter, (Ann Arbor, Michigan: Center for Japanese Studies, the University of Michigan, 1993), 99–103.

7. For details, see Murai Yasuhiko, "Rikyu's Disciples," *Chanoyu Quarterly* 66 (1991), 7–35.

8. *Chado Koten Zenshu*, vol. 5 (Kyoto: Tankosha, 1956), 232–33.

9. According to the "*Metsugo*" portion of the *Nanboroku*, Rikyu is said to have predicted his posthumous role as protector of tea, saying: "One hundred years after my bones will be covered with mud and my soul dissatisfied, I will become the tutelary deity of tea and, I am sure, the Buddha's and patriarchs will lend me their power." In *Chado Koten Zenshu*, vol. 4, 266.

10. *Matsudaira Fumai Den*, vol. 1 (Tokyo: Keibundo Shoten, 1918), 103–4. Matsudaira Fumai deplored the state of tea in his generation and, in his *Kokin Meibutsu Ruiju*, recommended a thorough study of the past. He aspired to revitalize tea through the use of authentic utensils and rejected those of obscure or unknown provenance. The respect for authentic utensils, he held, would bring a new respect to the tea traditions.

11. The *Chado Benmosho* of 1690, printed in *Chado Zenshu*, vol. 12 (Tokyo: Sogensha, 1889; *Chado Yoroku* of 1691, a copy of which exists in the library of Kyoto University Library); and *Rikyu Chadogu Zue* of 1701, a copy of which exists in the library of Kyoto University.

12. The *Chanoyu Sandenshu* of 1695, including oral traditions of Rikyu, Furuta Oribe, and Kobori Enshu, a copy of which exists in the library of Kyoto University; *Chanoyu Hyorin Taisei* of 1697, nine volumes of which are in the collection of the Imabari Kono Bijutsukan Museum under the title *Chanoyu Hyorin Taisei*; and *Chanoyu Rokusosho Denki* of 1702, printed in *Cha to Chajin*, part 1 (Tokyo: private publication by Isono Keisuke, 1991).

13. *Ekiken Zenshu*, vol. 1 (Tokyo: Ekiken Zenshu Kankobu, 1910), 2.

TEAHUTS AND TEA ROOMS

1. Under the patronage of warriors such as Sasaki Doyo, tea shifted from the religious to the warrior class.

2. Governor in charge of the military government.

3. *Taihei Ki*, in *Nihon Koten Bungaku Taikei*, vol. 36 (Tokyo: Iwanami Shoten, 1962) 443–44. According to the *Taihei Ki*, he offered hundreds of monkey skins to his followers and sent them off with a caged nightingale for each one. *Taihei*

Ki, part 2, *Nihon Koten Bungaku Taikei*, vol. 35 (Tokyo: Iwanami Shoten, 1971) 339.

4. *Muromachi Dono Gyoko Okazari Ki*, in *Higashiyama Gomotsu* (Tokyo: Nezu Bijutsukan/ Tokugawa Bijutsukan, 1976). This text was copublished in a catalogue on the occasion of the exhibition of the same title held in 1976. The *Muromachi Dono Gyoko Okazari Ki* is not to be confused with the *Okazari Sho* in *Chado Koten Zenshu*, vol. 3, or the *Eikyo Kunen Jugatsu Nijuichinichi Gyoko Ki* published in *Gunsho Ruiju*, vol. 3, Teiobu, which describe the same imperial visit.

5. Ibid., 468.

6. People could be lavishly rewarded for winning contests.

7. *Chado Koten Zenshu*, vol. 3, 68.

8. Rikyu, too, preferred the dark tearooms. Therefore he deviated from his predecessor Jo'o, who built a tearoom with paper walls, and preferred the darker clay walls. He was the first to build a south-facing tea hut while strictly controlling the amount of light allowed to enter with small latticed paper windows. Rikyu designed his Taian (Waiting [for Hideyoshi] Hut), originally built at the Yamazaki Castle and later rebuilt at Myokian temple a short distance toward the south of Kyoto, in the years 1582 to 1584 just after his lord, Toyotomi Hideyoshi, had defeated his rival Akechi Mitsuhide (1528–82). Rikyu mixed pieces of straw five or six inches long with the clay of the walls, creating a dark, somber effect. Like the modern writer Tanizaki Junichiro (1886–1965), who wrote an essay entitled "In Praise of Shadows" in Rikyu's opinion, darkness created a better effect than an excess of light. Since the Heian period, Japanese found beauty in the vague contours of darkness, mist, and rain. In designing his three-and-three-quarter-mat tea hut, Furuta Oribe continued Rikyu's tradition but added his own taste: he built a small window at the side of the tokonoma in order to throw some light on the scroll.

    Windows came to identify tea huts: there are the so-called "six-window huts" and "eight-window huts (*hassoken*)." Well-known examples are the Hassoken of the temple Manjuin, the Shokintei of the Katsura Imperial Villa, and the Hasso no Seki in Nanzenji temple's Konchiin subtemple. The latter's name, "Eight-Window Tearoom," refers perhaps to its original design, since today it has only six windows. The number six refers to the Buddhist concept of the six sensory organs: eyes, ears, nose, tongue, body, and mind. The number eight refers to the same, but counts the eyes and nose as two. The tea room therefore represents the senses; it is a kind of human body complete with all its sensory organs. Like Buddhism, tea tries to control these organs. If left uncontrolled, these sensory organs take over; the eyes and then the mind become preoccupied with a superficial pursuit of beauty, whereas tea seeks a unity of physical and spiritual beauty. The mind should control and prevent the six senses from becoming dominant. In the tea room, the mind should control everything and generate harmony among the senses, preventing any single one from dominance.

9. If the shutters were opened, these rooms were large halls open to the outside. The interior space was interrupted only by the posts supporting the roofs.
10. Cooper, "The Early Europeans and Tea," 124.
11. The writer Endo Shusaku briefly mentioned these notions in "*Roji ni tsuite no Gimon*," *Tanko*, vol. 39, no. 10 (October 1985) 82–83.
12. *Socho Nikki*, vol. 30-123-1 of Iwanami Bunko (Tokyo: Iwanami Shoten, 1975) 92.
13. Cooper, "The Early Europeans and Tea," 125.
14. Ibid., 122.
15. *Chado Koten Zenshu*, vol. 6, 102–3.
16. Sen Soshitsu, "Four and One-half Mats," *Chanoyu Quarterly* 22 (1979), 5.
17. Sen Soshitsu, "Scraps of Paper, Bits of String," *Chanoyu Quarterly* 37 (1984), 5.
18. Sen Soshitsu, "Ma: A 'Usefully Useless' Thing," *Chanoyu Quarterly* 46 (1986), 5.
19. *Chado Koten Zenshu*, vol. 4, 416.
20. Cooper, "The Early Europeans and Tea," 122.
21. Sen Soshitsu, "Purity in the Roji," *Chanoyu Quarterly* 64 (1991), 5.
22. Sen Soshitsu, *Hitowan no Ocha kara* (Tokyo: Gakushu Kenkyusha, 1983), 185.
23. Sen, "Purity in the Roji," 6.
24. Sen Soshitsu, "A Lesson from a Leaf," *Chanoyu Quarterly* 50 (1987), 5.

TEA UTENSILS

1. *Cha no Shintai*, 95, 148, 185.
2. Sen Soshitsu, "Bokuseki Are Foremost," *Chanoyu Quarterly* 68 (1992), 5.
3. *Chado Koten Zenshu*, vol. 2, 281–403.
4. *Chado Koten Zenshu*, vol. 6, 96.
5. The custom of naming utensils particularly favored by their owners is in fact an ancient practice. The "Saeda" (Small Branch) flute the emperor Toba gave to Taira no Tadamori passed hands to Tsunemori and, ultimately, to Atsumori, who took it into battle and his tragic death in 1184. Kobori Enshu often named his utensils in reference to poems of the famous collections *Kokinshu* of 905 and *Shinkokinshu* of 1205. For example, he named a Seto tea caddy "Asukagawa" (River Asuka), an image of mutability used in ancient poetry: "Yesterday" we say / And "today" we live, but still / Months and days pass by / As smoothly and quickly as / The waters of Asuka River. (See Yagi, Ichio, "Uta-mei: The Poetic Names of Tea Utensils," *Chanoyu Quarterly* 83 (1996), 16–39.
6. Printed in *Chado Koten Zenshu*, vol. 2, 405–501.

7. Sugimoto Hayao, *Sen Rikyu to sono Shuhen* (Kyoto: Tankosha, 1970), 322.

8. *Chado Koten Zenshu*, vol. 3, 27.

9. Ibid., 30.

10. Cooper, "The Early Europeans and Tea," 112-13.

11. Ibid., 114.

12. Ibid., 114–15.

13. Ibid., 124.

14. Ibid.

15. Ibid., 128–29.

16. Ibid., 115.

17. Ibid.

18. Ibid., 116-17.

19. *Bunrui Sojinboku* in *Nihon no Chasho*, Toyo Bunko, vol. 201 (Tokyo: Heibonsha, 1971), 279.

20. Cooper, "The Early Europeans and Tea," 125. Rodrigues realized that what seems so natural in tea huts and gardens was expensive and had to be brought sometimes from far distant places. "Then there is the garden, for which they make search in remote areas for trees of certain shape and fashion; the stepping stones too are expensive, for although they look as if they are there quite naturally, in fact they are sought for in distant places." (Ibid., 126.)

21. *Chado Koten Zenshu*, vol. 11 (Kyoto: Tankosha, 1956), 137.

22. Sen Soshitsu, "The Pure Heart," *Chanoyu Quarterly* 30, 5–6.

23. *Cha no Shintai*, 227–28.

24. Printed in *Chado Koten Zenshu*, vol. 7 (Kyoto: Tankosha, 1956), 1-460.

25. Printed in *Chado Koten Zenshu*, vol. 8 (Kyoto: Tankosha, 1956), 115-429.

26. Printed in *Chado Koten Zenshu*, vol. 9 (Kyoto: Tankosha, 1956), 1–491.

27. *Chado Koten Zenshu*, vol. 4, 10.

28. Sen Soshitsu, "Remembrances of My Father and Mother," *Chanoyu Quarterly* 35 (1986), 6.

29. Sen Soshitsu, "*Hyakka no Haru*," *Tanko* 51, no. 4 (1997) 22–23.

30. Sen Soshitsu, "The Spirit of Tea Is Global," *Chanoyu Quarterly* 71 (1992), 5.

31. Sen Soshitsu, "An Art of the Seasons," *Chanoyu Quarterly* 31 (1982), 5.

32. By Du Fu. In *Kanbunsen* (Tokyo: Kyoiku Tosho, 1964), 33.

33. By Du Fu. *Du Fu Shi Xuan* (Hong Kong: San Lien Shu Bien, 1984), 123.

34. Sen, "Bokuseki are Foremost," 5.

TEA PROCEDURES

1. *Cha no Shintai*, 173, 4.

2. Sen Soshitsu, "Seeking the Spirit," *Chanoyu Quarterly* 55 (1988), 6.

3. Sen Soshitsu, "Pause and Reflection," *Chanoyu Quarterly* 29, (1981), 6. Although musically different, these rhythms can be compared with the three movements in Western music, such as, for example, andante, allegro, and presto.

4. Shimizu Hajime, "The Alcove," *Chanoyu Quarterly* 3, (Autumn 1970), 5-6.

5. *Chado Koten Zenshu*, vol. 4, 420

6. Sen, *Tea Life, Tea Mind*, 32–33.

7. *Chado Koten Zenshu*, vol. 10, 299.

8. Sen Soshitsu, "The Tea Experience Called *Chaji*," *Chanoyu Quarterly* 69 (1992), 6.

9. Sen Soshitsu, "A Dream Remembered," *Chanoyu Quarterly* 26 (1981), 5–6.

10. Sen Soshitsu, "The Pure Heart," 5.

TEA FOOD

1. The opulence and arrogance of banquets in this period is exemplified in the following long verse, attributed to the doboshu Soami: "Now they get down to the meal / Raw fish, chicken, and everything else. / They lift the lids with haste, / And grab with bare hands / The raw-smelling dishes, / These overindulgent, gluttonous people. / The beautifully laid-out dishes / They turn upside-down and spill around. / They even crunch on the bones, / Mixing many things in their mouths, / Using their chopsticks in the wrong way. / Their chatter is mingled with songs,/They prattle about the most trivial subjects; / Their voices rise as they compete, / Each pretending to know everything. / They take no note of prearranged times. / Lifting up the large sake cups, / They force themselves to drink / Much more than they are capable of, / Till their behavior becomes undignified." From Tsutsui Hiroichi, "From Kaiseki to Kaiseki," *Chanoyu Quarterly* 50 (1987), 46. A reprint of the original text can be found in *Chado Bunka Kenkyu*, vol. 1 (Kyoto: Urasenke Konnichian Books, 1974).

2. *Chado Koten Zenshu*, vol. 3, 50.

3. *Chado Koten Zenshu*, vol. 6, 10.

4. Sen Soshitsu, "A Cold Episode," *Chanoyu Quarterly* 56 (1988), 5–6.

5. Ibid., 6.

6. *Chawa Shigetsu Shu* in *Nihon no Chasho*, vol. 2, Toyo Bunko, vol. 206 (Tokyo: Heibonsha, 1972) 16–17.

7. Sen Soshitsu, "Understanding Samadhi through Chanoyu," *Chanoyu Quarterly* 45 (1986), 6.

8. Cooper, "The Early Europeans and Tea," 127–28.

9. Included in *Furuta Oribe Chasho*, vol. 2 (Kyoto: Shibunkaku, 1984), 31–174.

10. A dish of sliced fish or shellfish seasoned in vinegar.

11. Yamada Sohen, one of Sotan's disciples wrote on the subject, "When there is

something one dislikes, one must not touch it with one's chopsticks. When one has touched it, one must eat it all." *Yamada Sohen Zenshu* (Kamakura: Yamada Sohen Zenshu Kanpukai, 1958), 84.

12. *Honkoku Edo Jidai Ryoribon Shusei*, vol. 3 (Kyoto: Rinsen Shoten, 1988), 46. See also Tsutsui Hiroichi, "The History of the Kaiseki Meal," *Chanoyu Quarterly* 78 (1994), 46.

13. From the *Uso Shu Shikan Sho*, quoted in Tsutsui Hiroichi, "From Kaiseki to Kaiseki," *Chanoyu Quarterly* 50 (1987), 52-54. I owe most of the above information to Tsutsui Hiroichi's articles.

14. Cooper, "The Early Europeans and Tea," 127.

15. *Chawa Shigetsu Shu*, in *Chado Koten Zenshu*, vol. 10, 205-6. See also Sen, "A Cold Episode," 6.

16. Sen, "The Experience Called *Chaji*,"5.

17. Sen Soshitsu, "One-sided Tea People," *Chanoyu Quarterly* 42 (1985), 5.

18. For more details on this subject, see Gretchen Mittwer, "Tea Sweets: A Historical Study," *Chanoyu Quarterly* 57 (1989), 18-34.

TEA FLOWERS

1. *Cha no Shintai*, 49, 134.

2. *Chado Koten Zenshu*, vol. 4, 7.

3. Ibid.

4. Ibid.

5. Sen Soshitsu, "Flowers in the Tearoom," *Chanoyu Quarterly* 58 (1989), 5.

6. Ibid.

7. Sen Soshitsu, "The Japanese Art of Arranged Flowers," Chanoyu Quarterly 60 (1989), 14.

8. Sen, "Flowers in the Tearoom," 6.

FOURTEEN GENERATIONS OF GRAND TEA MASTERS

1. Sen Soshitsu, "A Dream Remembered," *Chanoyu Quarterly* 26 (1981), 5.

2. Like tea utensils, swords were also given names—this one was probably named because it had once belonged to shogun Ashikaga no Yoshimitsu.

3. In 1595, Shoan went to Daitokuji to ask priest Senkaku Soto about the meaning of the name Rikyu literally, "Putting Fame to Rest"), a symbolic expression of his will to continue the Senke family in Kyoto (rather than in Sakai) and to establish it as Rikyu's legitimate lineage.

4. A temple built at the behest of Ishida Mitsunari and Asano Nagamasa, two prominent sixteenth-century warlords.

5. *Nihon no Chasho*, 41.

6. "Rear" and "Front" derive from Sotan's will, which divided Rikyu's Kyoto property into front and rear portions, the latter being associated with wabi tea and the former more with daimyo tea.

7. Reprinted in Sen Sosa's *Omote Senke* (Tokyo: Kadokawa Shoten, 1965), 96.

8. I will henceforth use the *-sai* titles in the biography of each tea master, even when referring to events prior to the receipt of that title.

9. The Noh theater, too, fell on hard times; the Kanze school did not have a single student. When the public school curriculum was created, none of the traditional arts were included. Music, for example, was taught entirely as a Western subject.

10. *Cha no Shintai*, 168.

11. Nagai Minoru, *Jijo Masuda Takashi-O Den* (Kamakura: Nagai Minoru, 1929), 217. See also *Daichajin Masuda Don'o* (Tokyo: Gakugei Shoin, 1929), 41–47ff.

12. The "ten artisans" (jusshoku) were ten families that had manufactured tea utensils for the grand masters for many generations.

13. I am indebted for the above information to Murai Yasuhiko, Sen Sosa, and Sen Soshitsu, *Chado no Genryu, Rekishi-hen* (Kyoto: Tankosha, 1983), 83–112, and to *Cha no Shintai*, 231–35 ff.

THE LIFE OF HOUNSAI

1. The quotations in this chapter are from Sen Soshitsu, *Ocha o Dozo— Watakushi no Rirekisho* (Tokyo: Nihon Keizai Shimbunsha, 1987) and from vols. 71 (1992) through 87 (1997) of *Chanoyu Quarterly*.

2. Sen, "Remembrances," 5.

3. Sen Soshitsu, "Form in Chanoyu," *Chanoyu Quarterly* 24 (1980), 5.

4. *Chado Koten Zenshu*, vol. 4, 319–20.

5. Sen Soshitsu, "Tea for the World," *Chanoyu Quarterly* 47 (1986), p.5.

6. Sen Soshitsu, "*Ryusui Kandan Nashi*," *Tanko* 40, no. 7 (July, 1986), 22.

7. Sen, "Remembrances," 5.

8. Sen Soshitsu, "The Attainment of Inner Tranquility and Strength," *Chanoyu Quarterly* 28 (1981), 5.

9. Sen Soshitsu, "Japanese Culture and the Global Environment," *Chanoyu Quarterly* 72 (1993), 8. *Otemae* means "serving tea."

10. Sen Soshitsu, "*Mosukuwa no Chanoyu*," *Tanko* 42, no. 11 (November, 1988), 22–23.

11. Sen Soshitsu, "Everyday Life and the Heart of Tea," *Chanoyu Quarterly* 11 (1975), 1.

12. Sen Soshitsu, "*Kokusaiteki Jinzao o*," *Tanko* 40, no. 11 (November, 1986), 26–27. For similar thoughts, see also Sen Soshitsu, "*Shin no Kokusaijin*," *Tanko* 52, no. 6 (June, 1998) 22–23.